Embrace who you are.

Xray your meaning.

Perceive a better you.

Reset your mind.

Explore your possibilities.

Save yourself.

Strengthen your happiness.

Improve your environment.

Offer your positivity.

Number your blessings.

Share your knowledge.

Poetry.
Personal.
Perspectives.

JD

EXPRESSIONS Poetry. Personal. Perspectives. © 2017, Revised and Reprinted ©2025 by JD

All copyrights are retained by their respective owners. Images owned by other copyright holders are used here under the guidelines of the Fair Use provisions of United States Copyright Law. The texts included in this publication are presented solely for purposes of entertainment, awareness, reflection, and inspiration.

No part of this book may be copied, stored, retrieved, or transmitted in any format or by any means, whether electronic, mechanical, or otherwise, without the express prior written permission of the author.

For inquiries regarding comments or permission to use any portion of this book, please contact the author via E-mail:janetbexpressions@gmail.com

Printed in the United States of America

Self-Published in the United States of America ISBN: 978-0-9990926-2-0

Library of Congress 5756677904

Illustrations courtesy of Pixabay.

This poetry book is a blend of fiction and creative nonfiction. Any similarities to actual events, incidents, people (living or deceased), locations, or organizations are either the result of the author's imagination, used fictitiously, or entirely coincidental.

Every effort has been made by the author and the publishing company to ensure the accuracy of the information contained in this book at the time of publication. However, neither the author nor the publishing company accepts responsibility for any loss, damage, or disruption caused by errors or omissions, whether accidental or otherwise.

This poetry collection is inspired by personal reflections, experiences, insights, and imaginative musings, offering a rich tapestry of perspectives and observations. The book is divided into seven sections, each introduced with a narrative-style paragraph that weaves together personal quotes, viewpoints, and poem titles. To deepen the reader's connection to each poem, a personal quote accompanies every piece, enhancing its meaning and underscoring its message. My hope is that this collection resonates with you, sparking enjoyment, thoughtful contemplation, and a sense of relatability.

CONTENTS

Reflections	1
Poem Titles Narrative	2
Poems	3
SINS	15
Poem Titles Narrative	16
Poems	17
Push Adversity	25
Poem Titles Narrative	26
Poems	27
Challenge Mindset	47
Poem Titles Narrative	48
Poems	49
Sex & Love	68
Poem Titles Narrative	69
Poems	70
Betrayal	87
Poem Titles Narrative	88
Poems	89
An Invested You	104
Poem Titles Narrative	105
Poems	106
Additional Personal Quotes	135

Reflections

"Keep your mind open to things that flatter your intelligence
and not to things that flatter your incompetence."

Reflections are what help us to look closer at ourselves and critique (hopefully), what we have done, what we need to improve, and how we make sense of the world to know who we are. As we reflect on who we are, we should learn something new about ourselves and understand why we do what we do and what makes us unique in our experiences. Like you, I've searched for direction in my life. I've taken paths that forced me to look at different factors that influenced and shaped who I am. I am always a work in progress. I am a student of life. I've learned to reflect on ways and choices in life to cope, to connect, to commit, and to change.

Why don't you take a moment to reflect on factors that influenced and shaped your choices, experiences, relationships, and learning. You might have asked yourself questions like, Who am I? What makes me happy? What is the meaning of my life? What is my origin? What is my purpose? What makes me relevant? Why do I make the same mistakes? Why am I still single? Why do I like to be single? Why did I marry that person? Why didn't I marry that person? Why do I stay or why did I stay in a toxic relationship or job? How do I overcome my problems?

If you asked yourself any of these questions, or related ones, as I have, then you certainly reflected on things that are important for your growth. One thing that's important about reflections, regardless of its capacity, at some point, there should be lessons learned at least for those who want to change.

Poem Titles Narrative

I Am Blessed! to know that to *Raise Your Children*, whether you are a *Family, Friend, or Foe*, the *SELF* will always show itself. It may be wonderful to sit on *The Good Seat* and in the *Sound of Silence*, but sometimes you don't always see things in *Plain Sight*. When you notice *Time Knows* that *People Have Fallen* and they need to use *A Bit of Common Sense*, there will be days that will make you say *I Don't Have Time for That!*

I Am Blessed!

"A parent's journey can be long and bumpy but its travel can be blessed."

As a mother, raising children is never easy. You have to recondition to make transitions, conduct supervision to address issues, education, training, and give permission, be ambition to support their missions, be a magician to make split second decisions, be a clinician to monitor health including the right nutrition, and be a politician to oversee funding for living conditions and inform them about society's systems while being sufficient. And so, I am fulfilled by the thoughts of holding my children, fulfilled by the thoughts of knowing they were given. As a mother, I raised them alone and I asked God why my children had to be statistics of a broken home. Now they're grown, thankfully taking care of their own and although we may make ourselves or others statistics of something, I've learned to be a strong woman and a mother who raised my children without regrets, without guilt, but with genuineness, connectedness, and love to help them rise above. As a mother, I am proud of my children, even my grandchildren. I guess what I am trying to say, nevertheless of a mother's stress, I reassess my progress is because I Am Blessed!

Raise Your Children

"A family without unity is an easy prey for division."

Fathers, care for your sons.
Mothers, care for your daughters.
Parents, care for your children
cease letting children care for themselves
cease letting them seek to find underground
help. Is it right not to educate them about who
they are or keep the vicious cycle going
like it's a demanding repertoire?

Fathers, care for your sons.
Mothers, care for your daughters.
Parents, care for your children cease letting
children care for themselves cease letting them seek
to find underground help. Is it right to abandon them or
keep the vicious cycle going like it's a demanding stand in?

Fathers, care for your sons. Mothers, care for your daughters.
Parents, care for your children cease letting children care for
themselves cease letting them seek to find underground help.
Is it right to be cruel to them or keep the vicious cycle going
like it's a demanding rule to condemn?

Fathers and mothers you are parents in your own right,
even if you are a single parent Raise Your Children
in an environment of light cease letting children
raise themselves cease letting them seek
to find underground help.

Family, Friend, or Foe

"Your character can develop by what or who you continue to welcome."

Family, Friend,
or Foe which one do you know?
Those who have an honest heart,
a trusted one, or one who disappears to take care
then expect praise as mommy or daddy or person of
the year. Family, Friend, or Foe which one do you know?
Those who get high or drink all day, then call you wanting
something and telling stories about nothing or about
yesteryears until you cheer. Family, Friend, or Foe
which one do you know? Those who know that
friendship is so dear they'll be the first to prepare
as a friend who is undeniably sincere.
Family, Friend, or Foe which one do
you know? Those who adhere to
hidden agendas and appear
connected and debonair
yet they are nothing more
than the devil's right hand
peer. Family, Friend, or Foe
which one do you know? Those who
owe you money always borrow and say
they'll pay you tomorrow or those who have
nothing to lose, have no ideas, or often interfere
and disrupt your atmosphere. Family, Friend, or Foe
which one do you know? Those who are holier than
thou never practice what they preach or those
who always give a speech and volunteer to
domineer. Family, Friend, or Foe
which one do you know?

SELF

"Your ways of living determine your rise and fall."

Sacrifices are made to rise on platforms.

Exposures good or bad conforms.

Lessons move in darkness and light. How come?

Foundations are not always common,

some forgotten, some cause problems,

some hit rock bottoms, and some are strong

and blossom. Either way, what influences

Sacrifices, Exposures, Lessons, and Foundations

can make the SELF wholesome to be made awesome!

The Good Seat

"Face oppositions with rigorous determination."

What gives you the right to tell me
what I need? You push your greed,
doctrines, perspectives,
directions, programs,
references of desires,
works, and relations
for my assimilation. You endorse your images
all day every day to dominate creating subconscious
thoughts training me for loss, then to be found on your cross.
Where's the freedom in that? Now, I sit here and rest in a space
where I can tell myself what I need so my identity is not erased. What
gives you the right to tell me what I need? You think you're discreet
to keep me in a box to trick me with unhealthy treats. I
can't accept that defeat. I must live in awareness of
my focus my peace my vision on The Good Seat.

Sound of Silence

"Your development becomes stronger when you are attentive."

Stop
talking.
Listen to
the symphony
in the air playing its strings
as the winds move with harmony
in its sound to vibrate your refinement.
Stop talking. Listen to the symphony in
in the air playing its strings as the winds
move with harmony in its sound to vibrate
your assignment. Stop talking. Listen to
the symphony in the air playing its
strings as the winds move with
harmony in its sound to
vibrate your internal
guidance as you
listen to the
Sound of
Silence.

Plain Sight

"A controlling system creates one perspective."

Something new
is coming our way.

It's going to be a world
event as one forcing everyone

to succumb to order lining us up
like ducks many will get stuck.

They want to own us. They show us
they can tag us drag us and bag us.

We are their pons on
the board, shifting

us like target moves for
controlled sites, pathways,

and materials that track us
through every coded digital.

They're watching and at any time
they can take away our rights and

despite how much we scream, kick, and
fight, we might want to keep our eyes open
to see that the plan is right in Plain Sight.

Time Knows

"Time is limitless, but your time is limited. Spend valuable time to liberate yourself and others around you."

It's time for
you to wake up
and reboot your thinking.
Time dominates conduct in
every direction of convincing
linking. Time shows you can be
in combat against yourselves in
combat with everyone else. Time
shows the smart, the wise, the
dreamers, the procrastinators,
the disorders, the offenders,
the fools those in between
who rules.
Time shows the disasters,
the survivors, the liars,
the puppet masters,
all lifestyle manners.
Time shows it waits
for no one so without
the armor of time on your
side you can backslide to the
zombie thinker like many worldwide.
It's not enough to shift thoughts you have to
act on organize and strategic moves to go beyond
a crisis to manage its resurface and negative devices.
Time shows all in the world of colors shapes and sizes.
Time Knows your voice and thinking are priceless.

People Have Fallen

"Question what you don't know. Question again what you think you know. Things are never what it seems."

People looking
like you and your
oppressors too are trying to

get over on you. They want your
friendship your company but they

too busy being a phony and violate you
expecting things to be as a ceremony.

They steal the truth and sell it to
many minds but with a twist
known as the truth of lies.

They manipulate the minds to keep
eyes blind by things advertised.
They keep ears deaf by
things supervised.
They keep spirits fed
by things antagonized.

The truth is People Have Fallen
with truth to know the truth of
lies as they also scotomize.

A Bit of Common Sense

"Sometimes we just don't use our natural born sense."

If you're a woman who complains that your man has too many children, then why add to his stock thinking you can put him on lock. If you're a man who keeps making babies and can't afford the costs, then why bring life when you know you fall short on child support. If you're a woman who sleeps around, then need help from authorities to find the baby's daddy because you don't know, perhaps you should cease all performances at the brothel show. If you're a man or woman who dates a cheater or traitor, then don't complain about their behavior when you catch that person with the neighbor. If you're a man or a woman who is the culprit for an affair and is jealous, then stop dating that spouse or partner and complain that men and women cheat... you are the one keeping cheating hearts upbeat. If you're a man who asks a woman to marry you, then don't bring baggage blues from baby mama and legal dues and cry out, "I don't know what to do!" If you're a woman who says there are no good men because you chose a few bad ones, then screen, assess, and select one that's not a mess. If you're a man or a woman who always complains about your partner or spouse and you want out, then why stay? No one is keeping you from a break away. If you're a woman who makes a sex tape or sends nude pics to your man, someone else's man, or to other wireless scans, then don't complain about your privacy when you invited society. If you're a man or a woman who ignores red flags, live in pretense, on the fence, or is dense, know that your experiences come at the expense of not exercising A Bit of Common Sense.

I Don't Have Time for That!

"Days are filled with annoyance, frustrations, joyful surprises, and stressful events, but days can be entertaining."

One Monday,
a young woman has an early
morning rise. She's awakened by her
ex-lover's cries but let me summarize.
She listened to her ex-lover on the phone knowing the
same script started with, "Are you alone? Are you with someone I've
known?" That's a warmup for an argument that grew full-blown, so here
its tone, "What's your problem waking me up early in the morning accusing
me of something. I can't believe you're asking me who I'm loving. You call
me looking for a confession then fall into regression to avoid facing your
indiscretions, obsessions, and transgressions." The response was depressing.
"There you go with your aggression. All I want is for you to talk to me. I'm
not trying to disturb your peace. I just want to know do you have
a man between your sheets?" The young woman released,
"I'm tired of your implications, you're a maniac and
I Don't Have Time for That!"

One Tuesday,
a father came home from
a long day's work all he wanted was to
get some rest. His son came into his room
feeling distressed and talked about his pockets empty
more or less. The father said, "Don't come in here with that
mess. You're looking funny and I don't have any money.
I'm tired of your begging. You have to help yourself and
don't start yelling or with the chitchat because
I Don't Have Time for That!"

I Don't Have Time for That!

One Wednesday,
a couple was having problems.
One said to the other, "You come in here
drunk, complaining, fussing, or cussing or all above
because you had a bad day. Sorry to hear that, but don't
displace and treat me as your doormat because
I Don't Have Time for That!"

One Thursday,
an older woman was talking
to a friend. She said, "What's wrong with
people rushing and pushing to get a seat or driving crazy
on the streets. I get to work the boss wants to meet some
workers are slackers so everyone feels the heat. Now, I have
to sit here and listen to the bureaucrat, and you know
I Don't Have Time for That!"

One Friday,
God said, "Thank you, Jesus! it's Friday and
the days that follow I don't want to hear any
spat or have anything to do with brats
because any day of the week
I Don't Have Time for That!"

Selfishness Influence New Seeds (SINS)

"What are your SINS?"

Life has a way of showing us that we are not always in control. Things and people contribute (intentional or not) to us being at risk, unsafe, victims, perpetrators, winners, losers, sick, healthy, poor, rich, educated, wise, and fools. You get the picture.

Whether people are good or bad, the limitations of moral judgment and the abasement of human life are sometimes undermined by the breaking points that manifest when a crisis, traumatic experiences, flaws, low self-esteem, frustrations, insecurities, blaming, or stressors become tangled in negative behavioral, emotional, and psychological responses. Sounds familiar?

That said, we live in a society that encourages tolerance for conformity thinking and behavior and find normalcy in dysfunctional relationships and negative communication and interactions. Despite the ugliness and evil in the world, if we want to stop justifying undesirable thinking and behaviors, we can try to stop giving it a pass.

Poem Titles Narrative

Everyone Is A Suspect! in display of *The Beast!* which attacks viciously when its *Smiling Teeth Bites!* When *Simply the Face of Greed!* have friends like *Sudden Rush!* and *Self-Rise!* the impact can be internationalized. Though people in the world are not always nice to others, sometimes you can abuse yourself in an *Indulgence Feast!* and ignore that to *Move Your Mind!* increases your baseline.

Everyone Is A Suspect!

"Nothing is stronger than the thoughts of your mind,
except for the actions that follow your thoughts."

Worlds of
illustrations
in peace,
illustrations
in war,

illustrations
in imperfection
through all doors.
The core of who you are
the core of who you know
the core of enigma, look close,
closer to find all exposure.

Like holders
of innocent eyes are misdirected by guilty
eyes that select victim eyes. All eyes reflect and cross
boundaries of person, property, and perspectives.
So, what's the objective? Listen, be vigilant to
the intellect, to the ignorant, to the
ambivalent mindset that freedom,
protection, and nature's beast
expected and unexpected
suggest people are not
perfect that's why
Everyone Is A
Suspect!

The Beast!

"A distant heart has no connection,
but a distant mind can be dangerous with anger."

Pinned up emotions,

weaknesses, selfishness, and

pathologies combined ignore accountabilities

and responsibilities of human behaviors

down the line. The innocent, evil, and guilty

alike move swift in their interests for the

sake of riches, indignation, fame or

meaningless claims.

Killing, abusing, and destruction

of life leave no one safe in the

end from its sharp knife.

Days and nights all the same
anyone can become a product of anger
inflamed. Around the world campaigns are
against human threats, hardships, sufferings,
and crisis all increase frustrations that create
more biases. In the end no one is release, not even the
police, because only the Creator can truly peace The Beast!

Smiling Teeth Bites!

"A person who has many friends thinks there are no enemies.
A person who has friends and enemies knows the potential of both."

I fought for you,
covered for you even
when no others believed in you.
Now, you turn your back on the things I do.
What happened to saying, "I'm here through the storms.
I'm here no matter who's wrong. I'm here even when your
status increases strong." Thought you were happy for me but your
deceit incited your dislike for me. Who knew you wanted to move on.

I Guess I was right, Smiling Teeth Bites!

You wanted all of me.
I never denied your agenda. I obliged thee.
Freely made sacrifices thinking that would have sufficed.
Didn't know I would be paying a price. Thought we were bind,
just had me blind. When I inclined, I believed you were my cheerleader.
Who knew your hidden mind wasn't benign, scary to think you're Borderline.

I Guess I was right, Smiling Teeth Bites!

Just to think you
enthused my heart, remember that's
what I gave. I never refused your love, remember
that's when you craved. We vowed not to abuse our trust,
remember that's how we agreed to behave so why would you
throw it all away because you're feeling some kind of way. Thought
you were innocent about my change. I didn't know you were green-eyed
every day. Who knew you hated me like a slave and had envy engraved.

I Guess I was right, Smiling Teeth Bites!

Simply the Face of Greed!

*"To profit by compromising your soul to misdeeds
will have you pay as a sacrifice."*

The sunrise
the sunset. Your
mind constantly scheme
to finagle gains by any means.
Even when you're at your best, you don't
leave anything to chance that just gives you no advance.
No matter how much you possess, still your untruthful and
corrupted ways comfortably prey on the vulnerable and
desperate exploiting them with no regrets for your
progress. Without a care no one is spared. You
show no mercy no integrity. Like a serpent
cold and calculating, your deception
is strong in building a nest
while making others believe
you have their best.
Along your quest
you think of
your next move
your next victim
your next competition
as you unleash your takeover
with venom and no redemption.
You are bold to stand alone, bold to
stand whole, bold to stand in control which
makes you honor your worth more than another's
soul. Eventually your demise stumbles showing no
escape but it means nothing. You say, "I only got caught
because I made a little mistake. Please give me a break!" Yet
you show no remorse for others' loss only for the respect of your
talented mind that planted the seed for your reputation that's
Simply the Face of Greed!

Sudden Rush!

"Eyes of the soul see its desire and
the flesh desires to fulfill its stimulation."

Open
invitations
lie beneath the
freedom of instant
gratification so easily
intrigued by the persuasion
of its ever so sweet temptation.
You say to yourself, "Glad it's not me.
In fact, it could never be me." But indeed, it's
your dark secret down deep. Like many others who
pursue the same desirable treats to play for keeps, you
imagine that you have an upper hand of being a silent
fan. Intoxicated by worlds of vivid and exotic themes, you
cannot resist the advertisement of nude cuisine all laid
out next to you, before you, behind you even while
you play peek-a-boo. Your heart races with excitement
anticipating the tastes of enjoyable body
enlightenment. Your eyes, your mind, your
flesh never cease to part from its mark
of hidden desires you thought you
never embark. You hunt every
chance you get to feel the
heartbeat of ecstasy and
romance of guilty
pleasures regardless
of the costs of risky
measures. And if this
is so! And if this is so!
then why deny that you
are extreme even in your
dreams of participating in
Sudden Rush! lustful scenes.

Self-Rise!

"A leader is made by others and listens to the cheers of wisdom. Lead in support not in the fall of pride."

Worldwide
beauty visibly
in a few. Many admirers halt
to conformity in wait of your view.
You are loving the mirrors, the eyes,
and the media lights all the same intertwine
seeing your images as a shrine. This makes you disdainful of others, and you give no attention to appearances
less than because you feel that's only made for victims
of an average scan.
Your beauty
insulted by mediocre faces
that make you flaunt visions
that massage and caress masks of
expressions in self-absorbing grace.
Enraptured by the deception of your
greatness, you devour glamorous
stares of your exterior repairs put on
a pedestal always believing you're
more exceptional and deserving
of top medals. Like a purple
diamond heighten by its
appraisal, your beauty is
of exquisite taste and
powerful like those
at a roundtable who
give absolute prize to
styles and riches full of
extravagant winnings and
labels. But take heed to hasten
your humble to do away with your
tumble. If not, no real favor will glorify
your arrogant stride that makes you succumb
to self-destruction pride and lies, so unwise, for the sake of Self-Rise!

Indulgence Feast!

"The focus on the belly increases risk."

Your belly
filled with delights from
consumption of appetite bites
crossing the line of immoderation
weighing heavily from your fascination.
The domination in your mind controlling
your relief in its comfort, in its joy,
in its pain, in its dedication.
What a stimulation!
Days and nights move in
your fixation suggesting a confirmation
destination as an unfortunate humiliation or
possibly causation. You say, "I have too many
situations motivating my justification that remedy
variations in my deterioration." What a great
self-evaluation, but here's a recommendation. "You
need another deliberation. Common observation
suggests you can suffer your socialization keeping
you in potential separation, isolation, or even
hospitalization. I'm sure that can't be good for
your salvation. Get help before you have
complications." Again, you say, "I can't
stop the hold, it's a relaxation."
Maybe so, but again I say,
"Get help. Don't console in
gluttony transformation.
You don't want an early
decease because of an
Indulgence Feast!

"Move Your Mind!"

"Embrace your worth. Don't delay your opportunities because you're afraid to move forward."

Why
do you sit
there like life is over
letting days and weeks
drift by controlling your mind,
body, and soul shaping your mold.
Who told you that you couldn't
break those chains? Cut those ropes?
Embrace those remains of hope?
Get up. Move! Don't let
yourself die soon.

Why
do you sit
there like life is over
letting months and years
drift by stagnating your growth,
purpose, and matter. Who told
you that you couldn't break those
strongholds? Cut those sorrows?
Embrace those tomorrows?
Get up. Move! Don't let
yourself die soon.

Why
do you sit
there like life is
over letting doubt consume
your exposure. Who told you
that you couldn't break those pauses?
Cut those flaws? Embrace those causes?
Don't lie there like a tomb. Sloth brings
nothing but doom. Get up. Don't get
left behind. Move Your Mind!

Push Adversity

"Adversities are inevitable. We must find ways to overcome them."

There are times when we try to understand the environment in which we select or are born into, and what we realize is that nothing exists on its own. Life is full of experiences that can change and shape our feelings, thinking, and behavior.

Life has a way of throwing us curve balls that expose us to different boundaries, limitations, and standards. We might not see things coming, such as the loss of a loved one, changes in our finances, or other daunting situations that can humble our experiences.

As adults, we are responsible for the well-being of ourselves, our children, and our environment. When adversity surrounds us in what hurts us, gives us pain, or tries to destroy our spirit, we must fight back against any strongholds that attack various aspects of our lives.

Poem Titles Narrative

We all experience adversities and there will always be days when we'll say, *We Miss You Too*. Sometimes *Life Knows No Boundaries*, and in its reality, it can offer pain, strain, and violates one's *Innocence*. Some may experience the element of surprise of being *A Hidden Me* or experience unpleasant *Headlines*. We live in *A World of Wildfires* that create many problems involving *Race* and *POVERTY* from living in an *Ingrain Society*. Some people may become damaged by *The Roots of Planted Seeds, Fabric of Patterns,* and a *Mirror Mirror*! effect indicating the need for *HELP!* even for a related problem of playing a dangerous game called *Knock! Knock! Let Us In*. This game is a product of the *Enemy's Custody*. The objective invites many souls to engage in *Nothing But The High!* a concoction of mixed ingredients that make it difficult for many to *Break the Poison*. Life takes us down different paths and some of us may fall and shout, *This Sucks*! The pressures of life can influence some to stray, inflict rage, or go throw a phase, and some fight for *Victory!* because in adversity *It's Very Real.*

We Miss You Too

"Life and Death live side by side and in its time each comes when it's called."

Going
through the
day in a casual way.
The doorbell rang, heard
your voice entered the room and
with delight we were glad to see you
that afternoon. We sat with you unknown
about your journey's flight no warnings gave insight to
your new-found release on life. We embraced the moment,
we joked, laughed, talked, hugged and said, "Talk to you later."
It was the usual enjoyment never suspected that you were
on your way to meet the Creator.
We can't believe it's true
we saw you yesterday
now you gone forever
We can't stop thinking
about all the days of
knowing you. We hate
that death sat by your
side and told you it was
time to say goodbye. We
had hope, but it bowed down
to the Angel's vote. We remembered the days
you laid in your place. It was hard to look at you with a straight face, memory retraced. The first day our understanding was astound. The second day our understanding profoundly bound. The third day our hearts sinking sad. The fourth day our spirit clinging mad. The fifth day our minds in disbelief. The sixth day our emotions in grief. The seventh day we were numb and couldn't grasp bereavement rightfully so, but we know you would say just let it go! We felt incomplete that your final earth day was no longer in our reach. You were a wonderful person and we know you miss us and want us to live life through. We Miss You Too.

Life Knows No Boundaries

"Life is like a predator that can eliminate the weak
and challenge the strong."

The life
of humans can
find purpose. The life
of trees can live for purpose.
Humans can embrace life being fruitful.
Trees can embrace life growing fruit. The
breakdown of humans results from the environment
and self-destruction. The breakdown of trees results
from the environment and human destruction.
Both humans and trees
can live in the same
or different
environments.
Both humans
and trees can
be violent.
Both humans
and trees can
live long and stand
strong. Both humans
and trees have the potential to
buckle to life vulnerabilities of things
gone wrong and Life Knows No Boundaries
when humans are faced with quandaries.

Innocence

"Let children be children.
"Let your actions guide them to a place of peace not destruction."

Why did you take their Innocence?
They are children who are to hold onto their Innocence for a little while longer!

They never invited you with
a smile. They said nothing.
They mind their own. Still
you sneak up on them as if
they are grown. Their tears
their fears fighting you off in
their bare skin still no defense
against your shifty hands and
manhood stance. Find your
match. They are not the ones
to welcome your gap. They
thought you were a friendly
stay. Wonder what their parents would say? You took
everything between their lay.
Got their minds in dismay.
They want to run away, hide-
away. They are a mess now.
They can't rest now. Got them
depressed now. Guess what?
It's time for your arrest now.

Why did you take their Innocence?
They are children who are to hold on to their Innocence for a little while longer!

A Hidden Me

"A buried truth becomes a living lie."

You told me
you hid who I am
because you snuck
around with a married man
and nine months later I was
born to be banned. I can't
understand if you love
me and suppose to protect me, then
why would you deny me the reality to
know who I really
am or to know
the possibility of
being connected
to a great kinsman?
I am almost grown still you
want me to leave it alone and stay
behind the scenes to never let anyone
know that I am my father's rightful genes.
Sometimes I daydream that one day while
I'm still in my youth you will tell my father
and me the truth. Don't you think that it's
time for you to take a stand and lift this
ban so I can know my family tree and
no longer live as A Hidden Me.

Headlines

"You will overcome those who violate you."

She explored
laughter and fun
and loved the decor surroundings, a
feeling of je ne sais quoi. She accepted his
advances as trusting until things went bizarre. There
were no warning signs he just twisted into savage mode.
Surprised to think he went down that road and made his actions
a penal code. He trapped her in the room. He acted like a rock star
vigorously stroked her body like a guitar. She pushed, struggled, kicked
and shouted stop! She couldn't restrain his force from getting on top.

She was confined behind enemy lines. He made her part of the Headlines. He put a knife to her throat, held her down ripped her through until he released his fluids, and then said, "Thank you." This stripped her away put her mind in a daze. Her tears ran down her face, her mind screamed inside, she had a frozen mind by the force of his Jekyll and Hyde. She was scared and terrified. She looked towards the sky and asked, "God, why? Please help me leave here alive." She was full of self-blame not knowing how to explain her insane shame. He smiled down at her as his dark eyes pierced her soul like a torpedo.

She thought, "God knows, I
can't let this go. He crossed the
line and had no remorse for his crime."
She made sure to report her attack during
prime time. Justice was swift and rumor has it
that his backside became a party line. Now, he
knows how it feels to be part of the Headlines.

A World of Wildfires

"No matter the size of the fire it never stops fast enough to end its pain."

There is a storm
moving around it makes
you attend burial grounds, keeps you
homebound, ruin backgrounds, shut down
playgrounds, induce meltdowns, promotes
shakedowns, separate environments from those
rundown, and poison health with compounds.

It's a merry-go-round.
You better turn around there's
no underground. Look around and see what's
heading your way, everyone is on its battleground
of spellbound. Are you safer than before? If yes,
then stick around and you'll see its many crowns.

It destroys
whatever gets in its
way. It destroys whenever
throughout the day. The storm
takes form without notice. It is focused,
very potent because its motive is to create
descendence to enforce dependence.

There is a storm
moving around. It brings
priors, suppliers, gunfire, crossfires.
It does not care about the choir or the
pacifier. Everyone and everything gets violated
because it's haywire not a campfire, and this makes it
difficult to escape when we're living in A World of Wildfires.

Race

"Too often people act on their idiocy."

How come you agree to
let me in until you saw my skin
my face? You mean I can't rent a space,
get a job at your workplace, eat at your fine
restaurant, shop where I want or even look
in your storefront unless you question me
with taunt. How come you agree to
let me in until you saw
my skin my face? You mean I
can't walk down the street, drive my car,
ride the train, or bus freely unless you frisk
me repeatedly. How come you agree to
let me in until you saw
my skin my face. You
mean I did something
wrong. I put my hands
up still you push me,
kick me, kill me when
you want with malice,
nonchalant. How come
you agree to let me in un-
til you saw my skin my face?
Let me guess, you probably
going to confess that your case
has nothing to do with my Race.

POVERTY

*"The way you think is how you understand.
The way you understand is how you learn.
The way you learn is how you understand
to cope in your thinking."*

Possessing no desire to reach mountains shift to dungeons because

Obsolete and disruption in your

Views are counterproductive, this can

Eliminate constructive thinking,

Ruin insight and eagerness besides

Threaten the environment and

You when you're coping in POVERTY, a phenomenon known as robbery.

Ingrain Society

"Your enemies are your enemies because they feel inferior to your worth."

Beatings, killings, and separations the same yesterday today and tomorrow ingrain. What's this helping hand with hidden resources, exploiting minds, and demanding conformity? It's pushing survival for degrading normalcy. Why do you help us with a false sense of security?

Beatings, killings, and separations the same yesterday today and tomorrow ingrain. What's this touch of iron and taste of substances for no productive health? Why do you distribute this waste into our place to liquidate ourselves?

Beatings, killings, and separations the same yesterday today and tomorrow ingrain. What's this warmth around our necks hanging us high?
We can't gasp our breath. Why do you wish our death?

Beatings, killings, and separations the same yesterday today and tomorrow ingrain. What's this we feel? Shackles from our waist to our ankles holding us down. Why do you provoke us with your hassle tactics breakdowns?

Beatings, killings, and separations the same yesterday today and tomorrow ingrain. What's this we see? There you go again trying to control us with your machines sending triggers of backseat psychological scenes.
Why are you afraid of our genes?

Beatings, killings, and separations the same yesterday today and tomorrow ingrain. What's this we hear? That's not our name.
Why do you want us to think miniature? That's not our signature.

Beatings, killings, and separations the same yesterday today and tomorrow ingrain. What's this perception? That's not our rightful identity.
Why do you try to make us hesitate our genealogy by teaching jealousy and false Egyptology? You desperately want to be like us but you denounce our features while you plagiarize our legacies and copyright our imageries.

> Beatings, killings, and separations the same yesterday today and tomorrow ingrain. Look at this Ingrain Society we live in that oppose our achievement but not our mistreatment.

The Roots of Planted Seeds

"The misery of others keep misery alive to destroy a safe place where thinking requires attention, understanding, and purpose for living a better life."

Comfort
rest not in a
place where
no meek
seek. Horns
of dark
souls greet.
Needs of
reforms halt
to transform
so tired
of these
quarrelsome
norms.
Walls crumble
doors tumble.
Visual beat
downs
harassments
and menace
surround. It's
time to get-
away break
free from
this
wretched
compound.
Oh, God.
Please!
help us
before we
malfunction in
pathological,
psychological
misdeeds living in a dysfunctional
environment of The Roots of Planted Seeds.

Fabric of Patterns

"Be mindful of your own and other people's moods."

Patterns running free in visions of
maladaptive behavior that exceeds so dramatic
it makes that person fail to heed pediatric psychiatric.
Patterns running free increasing disruptive leads so
erratic in tactics impede help during geriatric.
Patterns running free sow destructive
seeds making that person develop abusive deeds
such a tragedy, indeed. Patterns running
free give meaning to drastic needs
that proceed with paralyze returns,
poor concentration, and an avalanche
of concerns and foundation complications.
Patterns running free don't easily break
habits from its Fabric of Patterns
because they create frantic preventing
success when there's untreated manic.

Mirror Mirror!

"A broken spirit steals happiness, laughter, and life.
Let healing be renewed through the Higher Spirit."

Mirror Mirror!
Reflect on me. Mirror
Mirror! Who can I be? Mirror
Mirror! I have difficult sleep.
Mirror Mirror! Why do I
always weep?
Mirror Mirror!
I feel so sad. Mirror Mirror!
What is so bad? Mirror Mirror!
Life is no longer fun. Mirror Mirror!
Where can I run?
Mirror Mirror!
I have no appetite. Mirror
Mirror! When did I get smite?
Mirror Mirror! I have a siege mind.
Mirror Mirror! Why I am confined?
Mirror Mirror! My feelings are undergoing.
Mirror Mirror! What is knowing? Mirror Mirror! I
don't want to live. Mirror Mirror! When will they forgive?
Mirror Mirror! Hide my shame. Mirror Mirror! Who is to blame?
Mirror Mirror! I'm screaming inside.
Mirror Mirror! Where does my depression reside?

HELP!

"Listen to help when it calls."

He cries out, she cries out, they cry out, many of them cry out not believing anyone truly understands what they are feeling Is it a void? Is it a moment? Is it a comment? Is it an answer? Is it an action? Is it selfishness? All affect the deepest of the mind's eye, the emotions level, the behaviors fear of the daredevil. So, what does it really mean in the day, in the noon, in the darkest gloom? To some, it's the lowest of low the feeling of just wanting to let life go. Some try to understand to avoid the fall to internal overloads that burst into hidden conflicts banging, banging, and banging out those ugly thoughts feelings and self-arguments that lingers and sometimes rise to give you the middle finger. But in the awakening of the deciding scene of somber or dreadful exits, flights, or responses to life, which are harsh realities for some to know and invite, still some yelp in need and **H**ope **E**veryone **L**istens, **P**lease! for cries of HELP! in different degrees.

KnocK! KnocK! Let Us In

*"Mistakes happen and some mistakes are irreversible,
especially when lack of self-control becomes
the biggest debt to pay for your behavior."*

KnocK! KnocK!
Excuse me for waking you up this time of the morning, but my friend Alco last name Hol told me to introduce myself to you. My name is Canna last name Bis. I go by many names. I'm sure you know me as Weed, Marijuana, or Mary Jane. Anyway, Alco said you love that liquid company and you wouldn't mind another friend. Here I am at your disposal. I'm sure you'll like my feeling as I console you.

KnocK! KnocK!
Excuse me for interrupting you on your way to work, but my friends Alco and Mary Jane told me to introduce myself to you. My name is Co last name Caine. I go by many names. I'm sure you know me as C., Snow, or Candy. Anyway, Alco and Mary Jane said you like to make new friends. They said sometimes you can't wait for them to pick you up after work and sometimes you need a lift to work. Here I am to give you a ride. I'm sure you'll like me so much you'll become my bride.

KnocK! KnocK!
Excuse us for joining your party, but my friends Alco, Mary Jane, and Candy told us to meet them here. They said to introduce ourselves to all of you. My name is Molly. This is Meth, Dragon, Opioids, and Roids. Listen, there are so many of us just call us Drugs last name Destroy. Anyway, Alco, Mary Jane, and Caine said this party welcomes new friends. Here we are ready to dance with all of you. We're sure you'll like our feeling of highs lows flows, some might forget they never know while others will never let us go.

KnocK! KnocK!
As drugs and alcohol, we really don't excuse ourselves for being in your life.
We love being in the spotlight. We come to you morning, noon, and night. We don't discriminate, and for those of you who welcome our introduction, know that it's your choice. For others, you might become victims of another seductive voice. We are old, we are new, we are not obligated to be true to you. We'll make you look like a jock, put you in shock, make you stock up, even get you locked up. Depending on which one of us you embrace, or in combo, without a doubt we'll make you black out. So, if you're comfortable in your skin and willing to experience a world of fun regrets make sure to notify your next of kin.

KnocK! KnocK! Let Us In.

Enemy's Custody

"The delay of strength to change addictive behavior is a burden on the individual's stability and discipline but others will also pay a price."

Drugs, what is it all for?

You're just an invitation to many self-afflictions.

Predictions of consequences say you'll lead them to

convictions because of their addiction. You have

them paranoia, robbing, stealing, killing,

selling themselves, and lost

in excuses to support

symptoms of bad health.

Some will get help, some

will not, others will lose glory

as the story has it, life left them

in a hurry. Drugs, what have you done

to our friends, family, society? Your
cost is a liability to health, to support, and
to quality life. You proved your point. You're a
thief with strife. Drugs, they don't need your hold
your company or your puppetry. Release them
today from your Enemy's Custody.

Nothing But The High!

"Your goals should be consumed with resources to sustain quality of living."

They are running.
Their minds as high as
the mountain top. Carefree
about the world around the clock
nothing matters except more of their stock.
They are running. Their minds as high as
the mountain top. Carefree about the world
around the clock nothing matters except
the feeling when their high drops.
They are running.
Their minds as high as
the mountain top. Carefree
about the world around the clock
nothing matters except keeping the
stimulation nonstop. They are running.
Their minds as high as the
mountain top. Carefree
about the world around the
clock nothing matters except
that anecdote liquid and crush rock.
They are running. They need to stop.
Their minds as high as the mountain top.
Carefree about the   world around the
clock. It's Nothing   But The High! Doc!
Perhaps, they may need   a spiritual roadblock.

Break the Poison

"Choices have rewards and consequences. Don't choose to suffer."

Life pushing.

Pressures weighing.

Stressors peeling away.

Communication functions

sway by illegal substances every day.

Their responsibilities delay, risky behaviors display, lies

replay to keep euphoric needs trapped in repetitive coping

perceiving that everything is okay. They downplay reality and

remain in contradiction of their approaching doomsday because the decay in

their neurotransmitters made them lose their way. The time has come for them

to save themselves and live to see another day, maybe even their screenplay.

It's time for them to stop destroying, it is spoken for them to Break the Poison.

This Sucks!

"Sometimes situations remind us how important it is to prepare."

We're living on the streets can't afford anywhere to sleep nothing to eat our stomachs empty all week. We're running around trying to be survivors seeking help from those so-called providers. We're frustrated and confused because we thought we couldn't lose. We were hoodwinked.
We don't know what to think.
Heck, we need a drink!

We need shelter.
We need a job.

We feel down.

We feel stuck.

from being

struck and

This Sucks!

Victory!

"Taking off your shoes when you enter someone's home is respect. Taking care of your family is an obligation. Taking abuse from someone is never accepted. Don't enable abuse."

He breaks her heart.

He disturbs her peace.

He abuses her to her feet.

She tries to leave he made

her bleed. She becomes a

statistic and she knows it's time to

flee. She takes no more and head towards

the door. The Higher Spirit gives her a word. It

gives her strength in her spirit and courage to purge.

Again, he raises his hand to fight, lifts his tongue to

strike. It's his last stand tonight. She refuses to walk in

victim's shoes, it's no reward. Her worth is more than he

can ever afford. Oh! and by the way, her word is Victory! and

that makes her a survivor and makes him a prisoner delivery.

It's Very Real

"The universe will find a way to harm those who harm others."

Too many of our children and adults

are gone missing. Organs taken from the

young and old to sell for genetic transmission.

Human trafficking near and far adding to more

victims as they sell for high prices or
some based on commissions.

All of this chaos is breaking

down our social systems.

Everywhere I turn people are
losing their sanity to narcissistic
symptoms or splitting like they need an exorcism.
What's going on that no one is paying attention or care
enough to shut down the dogma traditions. Where's the resistance?

We are being dragged by twisted minds diminishing our existence. And

though we listen to the squeals, the raw deals, and what's being conceal,

at the end of the day, the higher ups see the ordeals and that all of this

mess in the world steals. It's Very Real.

Challenge Mindset

"An invasion of your thoughts should be filled with growth seeking quests not negative thinking that derail your life's blueprint."

Is there something about your mindset that scares you or challenges your self-worth, self-esteem, self-discipline, level of happiness, or cognitive dissonance? Is there something about your mindset that makes you cling to excuses or keeps you playing the victim role, wallowing in self-suffering, or blaming others for your shortcomings? Or is there something about your mindset that will allow you to accept that change can be embraced through self-empowerment?

Who you are in your character will show when you are confronted with stumbling blocks, snags, chaos, and stressors. Changing your mindset can involve exploring your awareness, observations, assumptions, choices, movements, and the root of the problems to adapt desirable behaviors and thinking. Behaviors and thinking are of the brain's design to think and know.

Thinking and knowing require recognizing that your mindset should connect to growth not disconnect. Disconnection sets the path for not seeing the values and aspirations to gain productivity in your life. To minimize any disconnection is to know challenges are real, but your mindset does not have to entertain long suffering when missing the mark of meeting needs and goals.

Essentially, to challenge your mindset is to understand that change, knowledge, and self-identity are meaningful when you are willing to bring forth a better you.

Poem Titles Narrative

True Colors present itself as the human mouthpiece that latch onto worlds of realities. This includes living in a world where you are in continuous link through the manipulation of *Live Wires* that show you various mindsets for what it was, what it is, and what it can become. Some may have *A Disagreement Inside* and become a *Misguided Self.* Their troubled minds stumble, their energy alters, or they even give *A Gift* of emptiness. When they *Self-Defeat*, they will disregard *Exposure*, expect for their own. *When you know who you are...!* sometimes *A Man and A Woman* can let differences disrupt communication, but there is also a lesson learned in knowing that *Wealth* can determine one's function and destination. Again, sometimes situations push you to manage your *OVERTIME*. Sometimes situations require you to ask someone *Are You Serious!* Overall, the mindset can be delicate and dangerous. If things don't work out, *Leave Your Cage* and *Unfold* to have *A Mind Like Water.* Learn *What You Soothe You Behold* in your *Shift!* because there are always *False Minds* that will make you *Kill It With Kindness.*

True Colors!

"The tongue is a powerful instrument. Be careful how you use it."

They are smooth
like the rhythm of percussion
beats that vibrate against chest walls
adding to spirits install. They drift through the wind,
levitate skylines, and motion across oceans wide and divide.
They are calm like a butterfly's beauty attest in its wings, impressed
by the essence its maturation brings. They gain admiration in
elation they spread through attainment paths, yet they grow in
submission to its predatory nature engagement wrath. They
are vicious like the wild and can disperse with intent
harm profile. They cut deep into the
heart of souls flowing deep into
the subconscious and conscious
dark holes. This is what you birth
when you exploit attitudes and
behaviors as worth. Know what
you bring to life is exposed in
words disclosed. Words impact
all lives in like, in dislike, in love,
in hate, in capture, in discover, in
destruction, in existence, and in extinction.
Words utter, "I am the Friend, the Enemy,
the Lover, the Mother of all showing its

True Colors!"

Live Wires

"A world of connections is a world of superficial and significant learning."

Touch our fingertips.
Touch our eyes. Touch our
minds. We love that twenty-four
hour addiction ride that got
us open wide. We can't let
go. It's taking control.
All hooked up on
more bytes
blinking
lights
and
sites.

It's a robotic connect that
makes us all objects. Respect the
space don't neglect or you'll regret its side
effects. Appreciate the outlets of collective
brains that exert innovations of life choices as
they contribute to generational gains. It's also scary to
think its loops push synthetics so pathetic open to gimmicks,
mimics, eccentrics, schizophrenics, and viruses systemic. There's
no limits, we all reap the creativity of technology Live Wires epidemic.

A Disagreement Inside

"Look inside yourself when you need to correct internal disturbance.
Look outside yourself when you need support."

Keeping your
eyes shut blindly aids
no guidance. Keeping
your ears closed unfriendly
produce noncompliance.
Keeping your voice open
bitterly speaks
as a virus.

Keeping your heart
beats coldly incite as callous.
Keeping your mind offensively
pollutes with malice. Keeping all
working together is a
forthright havoc.

Instead, keep

habits open to

new perspectives

to learn more than

A Disagreement Inside

with negative directives.

Misguided Self

*"Learn from those who add to your life and
learn from those who take away from their own lives."*

Look at who
they are in hiding
but soon they open
to obvious trace. Their
tongues utter kindness
because of their shyness.
They hold the minds
like a measure of fate
that moves at an intense
rate, but who knows what's at stake now that they are
irate. The truth is unglued by listening ears that heed
warnings of their flip flop mentality. Conscious
eyes heed signs nonstop of
their fake reality. Their
tempos altered by
unstable emotions
and behaviors showing
their personalities.
Layers of calm and peace are no
match for what they release when irrational
thoughts increase. Exhibition of insecurities flare in
outbursts on the street, temper tantrums fly like an ejection
seat. They run like a child profanity gone wild without reconcile.
This shows a confirmation of their tension not to mention
they need prayers intervention. Perhaps, in the comprehension
of themselves, each know their incompetence makes them
a complacent Misguided Self.

A Gift

"Give something that is worthy to cherish."

An
empty box
represents an empty mind.
An empty box
represents the giver who gives blind.

An
empty box
that's open finds no thrill.
An empty box that's returned
to the giver knows what's given could not fulfill.

An
empty box
belongs to no positive chat.
An empty box belongs to the
giver who gives according to its small hat.

An
empty box
is like a shadow in the
shades unknown to the eyes wondering
what's the point of this surprise.

An
empty box
is like the giver who is an
empty box inside knowingly disguises as
A Gift with the hope that the receiver will be satisfied.

Self-Defeat

"Complaining changes your process of thinking and builds consistency in making excuses. Stop complaining and process the things you can change."

Why do you find
ways to disregard meaning
with selfish blame? When you
can applaud meaning thoughtfully
with proclaim just the same. You are
your own problem. I try to be there
for you consistently still you live your
days filled with wasted air blowing
distantly and carelessly never
allowing any degree of
comfort to seek through
peacefully.
Why do you stay
true to victimization
given way to guilt, doubt, and ugly
reputation? I push you to build
confidence still you throw
away life with evidence of
tongues disgracing
your competence.
Why continue to live in
a cell like a defendant
down on a life sentence? One
day you'll stand still long enough
to imagine a new existence without
repeats of ignorance and failures to
complete. It makes sense to refuse
a backseat to small thinking and
mistreat to avoid persuasion
of your Self-Defeat.

Exposure

"True knowledge that's not recycle becomes useless to the next generation, and for those who are apathetic to acquire knowledge restrict their enlightenment."

What they see
in observation of
something deeper than the
knowledge of their own is
the observation of something
deeper than they have grown.
The observation of all those
books made them look.
They said, "We shouldn't
even be here. We feel so stupid, so excluded. What they
see in observation of something deeper than the knowledge
of their own is the observation of something deeper than
they have grown. The observation of the events on the
walls made them look. They said, "We have no
comparison with your high intelligence.
We don't know why we put ourselves in
a situation where we can't compete
with this relevance." What they see
in observation of something
deeper than the knowledge of
their own is the observation of
something deeper than they
have grown. The observation of
all those scripts made them look.
They said, "We want to understand.
We admire your enclosures but we're
afraid of the makeover." What they see
in observation of something deeper than
the knowledge of their own is the observation
of something deeper than they have grown. The
observation of their disclosures made them un-
comfortable to welcome positive Exposure.

When you know who you are...!

"Learn your strengths and weaknesses to avoid using methods that take away profound experiences."

When you

know who you are...!

there's no need to camouflage.

Treat others with regard don't waste

time playing the wrong cards. Appreciate

the welcome so you don't have to sabotage.

You cannot truly engage in others if you're far apart.

You must be connected not just present if you really want

a lasting heart. Don't seek out commitment to a higher

level thinker when you only can handle perspectives as a

wishful thinker. This will only increase frustrations not vigor.

When you know who you are...! there's no need to camouflage.

Treat others with regard don't waste time playing the wrong cards.

Appreciate the welcome so you don't have to sabotage. To
see the bigger picture is not to be impressive by memorized
scriptures but apply the spirit to face daily triggers. Don't try
to dominate others to listen to your egotistical monologue
to override their intellectual dialogue.
When you know who you are...!
there's no need to camouflage.

A Man and A Woman

"There are many ships: Wood ships, cruise ships, hardships, relationships, but there's nothing like friendships. Don't ruin it because of a minor discrepancy."

One day, two friends, A Man and A Woman, had a dispute. The man said to the woman, "You don't know what it is to be a man." The woman sarcastically responded, "You don't know what it is to be a woman and it's fair to say that we both don't know what it is to be a man." The woman saw that her friend was upset so she thought to encourage him to tell her what it is to be a man. The man, still upset, sarcastically said, "Let me run to Peru to figure it out and I'll get back to you."

Days, weeks, and months went by still no response. The woman called her friend and said, "Hey man, I thought you were going to tell me what it is to be a man." The man said, "I'm still trying to figure it out." The woman, reponded, "Come on man, it's been almost two months and you're still grudging our last conversation.

Thought we were friends..." The woman, sarcastic, "I guess I'll find a man to tell me what it is to be a man without having to wait a lifespan." The man sarcastic too, asked his friend "So, tell me what it is to be a woman?" The woman responded, "Let me run to Timbuktu to figure it out and I'll get back to you."

Wealth

*"A wise person plans to be educated.
A foolish person ignores to plan and lives recklessly."*

Tender minded and full of Rum.
All day long you were having fun.
Your life changed when you started getting
some. You stood tall and long getting it on the run.
But all that stopped when you got caught with a gun.
You said, "I was stupid for hanging out with the wrong
ones. Guess I should have listened to my loved ones about
living life in reruns." Now, you sit there waiting time and can't
help to think of the day your mother told you to stay in school
because it's the right thing to do. But
you felt school was boring,
you saw no point in exploring.
Now, you sit there waiting time
and can't help to think of the day your mother
told you to stay in school because it's worth to see
it through. But you felt school wasn't a guarantee
to be free. Now, you sit there waiting time and can't help to
think of the day your mother told you to stay in school to share
your themes. But you felt school was hypocritical and you became
cynical. Now, you sit there waiting time and can't help to think
of the day your mother told you to stay in
school to reach your dreams. But you
felt school was a waste of time
and your thinking caused
you to commit crimes.
Now, you sit there waiting
time and can't help to think
of the day your mother told you
to stay in school for no one else
but for yourself. But you felt school
wasn't cool and that made you a fool.
Now, you sit there waiting time and can't
help to think of the day you get out. All your
mother ever tried to tell you was to get your
education to help yourself and others and protect
your health because that's   a lifeline of real Wealth.

OVERTIME

"The need to stay on top takes persistence to maintain a position of comfort and in its existence, you are challenged."

Outer layers stretch the self exhaustingly, holding all your

Visions of the world tipping the edge of control slowly, forcing you to

Explore diversity and inclusion openly, confronting many

Realities everyday consciously, interpreting it

Through concepts and challenges excessively, influencing

Inner concerns stressing emotionally, knowing that your

Mind is exceeding limits psychologically, tolerating to deal with

Experiences to develop and grow, hopefully.

Are You Serious!

"Things that are not in your favor manifest unkindly.
In your decision to attack it, know that you can only
make you happy today and tomorrow."

Help me
to understand
why you are out here
fighting and ready to kill
over a man, over a woman? If he or
she wants to leave or cheat then let it be. You
see you must think before you take it to the streets.
Don't you know deceit repeats. Fighting and ready to kill
another is not going to change what happened. It can change your
status lower your standards make you look desperate and put you
in competition to be arrested. Help me to understand why you are
out here fighting and ready to kill over a man, over a woman? Is
it for respect, control, or both? Either way, fighting and trying
to kill just shows you have no growth. At some point you
have to learn to let it go. I understand you are hurt
and furious. Do you really want this to be a
continuous experience? If
so, Are You Serious!
Then you're an idiot.

Leave Your Cage

"Success is the adjustment of your thinking ability to reshape your life."

Living in mediocre got them sinking in minimum wage.

Living in downgrade got all sinking in disengage.

Living in a vacuum got us sinking in rage.

Living in average got me sinking offstage.

Living in inferior got you sinking in age.

Living in ordinary is not the problem.

That can change once we realize
we're sinking in engagement
to our situations that keep
us backstage.
Change your peception.
Change your perspective.
Change your page.
Leave
Your
Cage.

Unfold

"Time changes the process to explore purpose and
purpose to explore change is in the process of time."

Looking up at the sky raising your hands up high
you wonder what you have done with your life.
Just letting time pass you by you need to hold on
tight with all your might. You cannot lose your grip.
You know you need to commit to it. Admit it.
Own it. Nothing seems the same. You run.
You hide. You really afraid to
challenge the game.
Life choices made
you domain. You
dance around in your
mind with thoughts of situations
circumstances and disagreeable
change. You never stopped to think that one
day the growing pains of yesterday will hold
your freedom of tomorrow exchanged.
You say, "It's too much chaos.
Too much pressure. Too
much insane." I get it,
you want to stay
in your lane.
Your excuses
are through and
through so uncouth
so like you. Why do you follow
like a child without a point of view?
The time has come in due season to travel
the mileage in adult shoes. You have options
to uphold. The time is now for you to Unfold.

A Mind Like Water

"When you think broad, your thoughts can develop new possibilities."

It teaches that without it

people can die, with it, it maintains lives.

It teaches that no matter where you are in

the world it wonderfully spread to share in

its enjoyment. It also gives a chance to share

in its many circumstances of disappointments.

It teaches the power of its depth, of its

advances that are the wonders

of the earth.

It teaches that

when you look at the world to

know your place, what's in you can

be strong, what's in you can simply go

wrong. It teaches you to breathe and meditate.

It teaches you to find order, extend beyond its borders to

understand broader because you are A Mind Like Water.

What You Soothe You Behold

"The desire to reach new heights in your joy is an optimistic mind."

Like

a perfect day, the air still

with peace. No waves. No cares.

Just looking forward to

days of prayers.

Do not be

bothered

by worry

or trouble as long as

you place the right soothe

that calm beneath your feet and

in your soul to cast out all negative

controls. Your eyes know what's in your

mind as it holds, respect that and let go of

the uncertainties, insecurities, and overcome your

enemies. It will make you grow beyond to establish

the intensity of new ways to channel What You Soothe

You Behold without the austere in your atmosphere.

Shift!

"Old and new thinking can guide your transformation."

Dark talks shift the light.

Noises move shift the night.

Pull back shift the stride.

Push ahead shift the inside.

Scream quietly shift the soul.

Whisper loudly shift the control.

Walk it slow shift the start.

Rush it fast shift the depart.

Lift up shift the mind.

Stand still shift the grind.

Cry now shift the moment.

Laugh last shift the opponent.

Waste not shift the want.

Protect yourself shift the haunt.

Forward thinking shift the focus.

Cease doubt shift the hopeless.

Think diverse shift the mistaken.

Awake and Shift! before you're forsaken.

False Minds

"Sometimes we have to question who, what, and why we follow."

Many rush to
seek the word then to
find out that their leader can no
longer serve. Before that took place
they remember being criticized for their ways
being criticized for missing tithings several Sundays.
Is there something wrong here? They feel embarrassed that
their leader had an affair, so unfair, and she had the
nerves to tell them that they needed prayer.

Many rush to
seek the word then to
find out that their leader can
no longer serve. Before that took place
they remember being criticized for their ways
being criticized for missing tithings several Sundays.
Is there something out of place? They feel annoyed that their
leader is disgraced for an accusation case, so two faced, and he
had the nerves to tell them that they needed God's grace.

Many rush to
seek the word then to
find out that their leaders can
no longer serve. Before that took place
they remember being criticized for their ways
being criticized for missing tithings several Sundays.
Is there something undermined? They felt sympathy that
their leaders had to resign because they committed crimes.
All of this went streamline and their leaders had the nerve
to tell them that they needed guidelines.
Many rush to seek the word. They found
out their leaders can no longer
serve. They were criticized by
the very people who were to be
heard. This just goes to show
that following those who we
think are divine signs many
times turns out to be False Minds.

Kill It With Kindness

"To look for yourself is never within someone else. It's in you."

A bird I want to be.
A lioness I need to be. A sheep I
sacrificed inside of me because I was looking
for a kind King for protection, but he turned
out to be a killer for possession. A bird I want to be.
A lioness I need to be. A sheep I sacrificed inside of
me because I was looking for a kind King to answer my
questions, but he turned out to be a killer to quiet my
progressions. A bird I want to be. A lioness I need to
be. A sheep I sacrificed inside of me because I was
looking for a kind King to qualify, but he
turned out to be a killer whose
quarrels can be quantify.

A bird I want to be.
A lioness I need to be.
A sheep I sacrificed inside
of me because I was looking
for a kind King who wouldn't
quit, but he turned out to be a
killer with a permit. A bird I want to be.
A lioness I need to be. A sheep I sacrificed inside of
me because I was looking for kindness in the wrong place.
Killer King had problems with his P's and Q's, he misconstrued.
And so, it turned out that what I needed was not in him or anyone
but in me who moves like a Bird, have strength like a Lioness and
not sacrifice like a Sheep because I move above the mindless and
deceitfulness to Kill It With Kindness.

Sex & Love

"The body and the heart share in delightful experiences still each can be rivals."

Sex and love are human behaviors that transform our feelings into its own collective goals of intrinsic and extrinsic motives to feel alive, feel valued, feel good, and feel a sense of belonging to something or someone, even for the sake of status. There comes a time in our lives when we want more than random sex, arranged sex, or convenient sex. We want deeper connections that entangle our emotions into the equation of pleasurable and lasting thoughts.

We search for sensitivity, stability, security, and safety in our relationships. When relationships are going well, warm memories are stored for later retrieval and joyful feelings seem to last forever. Then, something or someone happens, and nothing is the same. Things fall apart and sex and love have episodes of disturbance or fade away leaving our feelings confused, bruised, and misused. Sometimes there are moments of nostalgic overtones that compete for our attention, and this may increase tension.

So, what does all this mean? It means listening to your inner voice and instinct to know your value and heed who and what influence your sex and love.

Poem Titles Narrative

A *Sexual Setting* is always ready when you want to enjoy the desires of *SenSual X!* or reach your *Destiny* but either way it's *Nothing but Sex*! This changes your perspective and *You Want Something More.* You enter a *Love Zone* that suggests *Love Is What You Think.* You might get caught up and have a *Crush* on someone for that *Long Awaited Kiss* that might fail to embrace many sunrises because things later grow *A Heart Apart*, especially when *Deceitful Love* treats you as a *Second Hand Love.* After some disappointments, you might believe there is no more *Life in Love* until love provides you with a *Stella Mate.* This may seem surreal. You might be flattered by one of many *Sexy Swirls* who make your spirit true making it feel like Deja vu. When you do meet your love, you might feel bold enough to publicize your *Close Ties.*

Sexual Setting

"Anything is possible when your invite is open."

S & M
are always
a little eccentric.
They are spontaneous
and sometimes can be
egocentric. When they think
you're a good fit, they will select you to
join their party skit. The invites can vary in
its delight. Its details are often right and offered
with candlelight so the expected guests can have insights.
Invitations are as follows but read carefully not
to misinterpret the motto.

For Adults
eyes only. No place
like hers. Date your
next Saturday. Fun time
at midnight. Theme is
adventurous. Bring
gifts to surprise
us because
we'll surprise you!
Dress comfortably for
all you can eat. Feel the music
pumping. Thank you and glad
you are coming because we will.

The guests arrived at the party. S & M greeted everybody.
The theme looked like a safari and there was plenty of Bacardi.
Everybody was having an enjoyable time nothing was short of sublime.
The highlight advanced with S & M dance romance that put all in a trance.
S kissed M lifted her gown and pumped to the music like a circus show clown.
For a moment the guests looked surprised. They couldn't believe their eyes
wide. They reread the invitation and realized they were inspecting
S & M's Sexual Setting!

SenSual X!

"The sacrifice of the body eventually sacrifices the soul."

Tonight's
admission
welcomes
all to release
the dragon for
submission and
dismissed all inhibitions
to commence deep penetration
of cognition flow without intermission.

Two
enters
the scene
looking to engage
they are amazed by
the Caramel Dominatrix's gaze so they
request a journey for an incredible fantasy lay.

They're
wrap with
protection working
each other like professionals
having a blindfold experience. What
a festival! But some would say it's unethical.

They tease
the mind, tear the clothes,
visualize the kind, let the hands
roam beyond boundaries lines. Gentle bites
and soft kisses freely find where they want to be.
They caress the nips explore with chains whips and vibrator
clips, taking turns sexualizing in exotic scripts. The excitement is a
mind blowing performance that's flexible and fun seXing tied down,
upside down, explicit until done. No one regrets two on one because it's
all for a night of memories making history in a SenSual X! documentary.

Destiny

"The flesh motivates the mind to seek its pleasures."

Her day was long and dreadful. Her mind wrestling to forget how stressful. Her body is craving, it's been neglectful. She needs a distraction to feel alive again. She disrobed to take a hot shower letting the water stream over her skin feeling comfort within. Her spirit peaceful her flesh sensual. She returns and extends across the bed looking up at the ceiling, it's a subliminal thinking about that traditional. She knows it's time
for his arrival.
He appears to
seduces her so,
kisses her lo,'
feels her libido.
She takes control. He slows his flow to delay his goal.
He stretches her motion to earn his promotion. Her
stimulation breaking free. Passion delightful, indeed.
He drives her
like speed,
a world
class sports
the best
in town
hands
down.
She's
ready
now for
higher
ecstasy
of his
agility
What
a climax
Destiny!

Nothing but Sex!

"We fail ourselves when we search for love in people who only want temporary gratification."

It was the

first. Thought to

give to love. Thought to

have it all. How could this be?

Never thought it give way to me.

He said, "It was nothing but sex!"
A quick dance. No romance.
Now I'm an Ex.
It was the first.
Thought to give to love. Thought
to have it all. How could this
be? Never thought it give way
to me. She said, "It was
nothing but sex!" No big
deal. No need to
appeal. Now my
ego's perplex.
It was the first.
Thought to give
to love. Thought to
have it all. How could
this be? Never thought it
give way to me. They said,
"It was nothing but sex!"
Nothing more. Nothing less.
Now I'm complex. Next time
expect that some people only
want Nothing but Sex!

You Want Something More

"Sex fulfills the desire. It cannot replace the deepness of love."

You are hanging
out in the clubs. You are
going to parties. You are going
everywhere just to meet somebody.
You don't care whether women
are from Baton Rouge
to Kathmandu or from
Puerto Rico to Rio. Your focus
is to charm and sex as many women who
can feed your ego. You believe women
can only hold your attention with sex.
You tell them what they
want to hear without any
intention of being
sincere. You feel
it's your duty to
entertain all the
beauties, the booties,
a fan club of groupies.
You are free and nothing
can tie you down you are playing
women like they are your personal
playground. Then there is a lovely one
who avoids your hound. She asked you to visualize
without limits. "What else is there after you use women?
What else is there besides sexing many? Would you share something
with meaning that's plenty?" You thought she was friendly and she made
you think about how much you were feeling empty. Sex is great but you
no longer want just playmates. You want someone to listen to you.
You want someone to come home to. You want her who knew you.
What you want is something that you never had before, something that you never allowed yourself to explore.
You Want Something More.

Love Zone

"Love is felt when the person shows their love is stronger than the obstacles that attempt to stop their unity."

A man's love is exciting.

A woman's love is expressive.

A man's love seems convincing.

A woman's love seems challenging.

A man's love holds visual.

A woman's love holds verbal.

A man's love seeks security.

A woman's love seeks stability.

A man's love like he's on a throne.

A woman's love like she's a backbone.

Both a man and a woman connect in their Love Zone.

Love Is What You Think

"People love through their reality."

Some people have
something important
to say to love, and they
hope love can accept
it as it's conveyed. Being
around love, it makes
them feel like their
hearts can move
mountains without
letting go or shifting
on grounds doubting.
Their eyes are
blinded by love's
beauty, it's so fine
they can't help to
think about love
within them, it's
a lifeline. They
know they sound
like fools but they
want to be love's jewels.
Their feelings are crazy,
they want to be hasty
with love making babies.
They know that's outrageous.
After all, they are courageous.
They know love is powerful.
They want to give love every-
thing allowable, it's so deserving.
It's so lovable. They hope they're not being gullible because love and they are compatible. It's love forever, a gift from above that makes them feel true love. They know they will never leave love like those who have no truth or happiness but only craftiness. They will keep love, treat love like Kings and Queens because strong men and women know the heart surrenders to love's pleasures. They don't run away from love's pressures. Though people are distinct in their love, they believe the truest of Love Is What You Think when love and the spirit are interlink.

Crush

"Be careful who you trust with your heart."

Like a high
school Crush
making you blush.

When you looked upon
those eyes you can't help
but get mesmerized.

Like a high
school Crush
making you feel plush.

When you're taken by the

hand you feel like you are walking

to the promised land. Like a high

school Crush making you rush to

hear that voice gush. When you're

listening to its heartbeat you feel

your body heat rising. Like a high
school Crush making you believe you
are the object to conceive but then you
think, "Am I being a little naive?"
Like a high school Crush.

Long Awaited Kiss

"If you're responsible in your decision, then let your private thoughts come true in the moment that do not cheat your happiness."

When

she saw

his face, his smile

made her feel good

all the while as memories
embraced his voice, her
body remembered
how she wanted
him as her choice.

When he saw her

face, her smile made

him feel good all the while

as memories embraced her voice,

his body remembered how he wanted her
too as his choice. He says, "They are forbidden it is
written." She insists as he couldn't resist knowing that
they are fitting. The two played like kittens that persisted in
a tale of twists that finally ended with a Long Awaited Kiss.

A Heart Apart

"Relationships are without perfection in compatibility, but this does not mean when unhappiness enters your heart, you stay to avoid being alone."

They picked up the phone several times to call each other. Doubt made them not want to bother each other. As they looked in the mirror and cried they saw that they died inside. Never had they wanted this to be their guide never had they wanted this to eat them alive. Though it did and they tried to find a way to survive A Heart Apart that knows pain and they know their love will never again be entertained.

Deceitful Love

"Honest love does not stumble and rest in the comfort of denial."

Deceitful Love
love speaks to connotation as if another chance gives to
romance sensation. Once more advances of attempted
love lend to no persuasions. You're not amused by
its immature invasions. Deceitful Love is conniving
and builds upon new beginnings with hidden
manipulation and lies thriving to keep
false hopes and dreams alive
while trying to grasp you
convincingly,
nice try.
It strives
to accept interpretation
that true love weight lift its purpose to
withstand patterns of exacerbation. In its act is
hypocrisy and that's a controversy, Deceitful Love
desires no prodigy of common sense strategies but runs
away with meaningless apologies. It simply pacifies to buy time
impressively because it has no spine to align with authenticity.
Deceitful Love shows no survival only denials hiding in wait pushing
visions down spiral ignoring to know honest love because it has
no moral values.

Second Hand Love

"Own who you are. Don't let someone else claim your worth."

You were taken by surprised
and entertained unexpected flattery in
disguise. Scattered feelings yield to gravity
heights and since you thought love was a
subscription right your heart danced to the
flashing lights. You set the tone. No deceit.
No lies. Feelings that were emotionally high
grew short-lived once you realized you were
a standby. The script of love exchanged the
range of meaningful relationships. It was just the
same old game. What a foolish heart to think you
were the only preferred. As it turned out your
significant love was sexing the chauffeur.
You didn't think your love was
an imposter, a pathological liar
planting seeds of disturbing
minds living in confusing,
You're not excusing.
You dismissed
infidelity desiring to
receive your affection
to quench the sexual
identity. You listened without
empathy because the one before you
was now your enemy. You didn't forgive
the broken code of unity, you rejected being
included in a Second hand Love community.

Life in Love

"The light of love lingers in its energy. To think that love will never come means you have no belief in yourself."

Shadows cast
a dark cloud over love.
Taking away your smile.
Making your heart bleed for a while.
Your mind crowded. Emotions flooded.
No one makes you believe there's a breakthrough.
You feel gutted, so cold-blooded! A selected few proven
its truth making you feel without.
You're tapped out.
You thought love
would hold you close, be a
friend 'til the end. You want a chance
to love again. You can't believe love
would throw you away 'til this day or
deprive you of cloud nine. That kind
of thinking almost made you consider
reading the guidelines to join love's
social lines. Down in your spirit you
can't let love die. You know
love must shine with a
sign to let you know
Life in Love is divine.

Stella Mate

"Love is worth the wait when your wait is worth the love."

Love, I want to get to know you,
but I saw you Betray the Heart from the start.
Before you show me that ugly face, give me a taste of your grace.

Love, I want to get to know you,
but I saw you Deceive the Mind just to get some behind.
Before you show me that ugly face, give me a taste of your wonderful state.

Love, I want to get to know you,
but I saw you Destroy the Spirit making emotions incoherent.
Before you show me that ugly face, give me a taste of your heavenly embrace.

Love said, "Some of the things you witnessed
cannot be disputed. It comes from those who are polluted.
Open the door your opportunity awaits you no more.
I am here to show you a true face, one that
gives you all your tastes known
as a Stellar Mate!"

Sexy Swirls

"When you feel a connection that encompasses your presence,
it's an undeniable experience for you to embrace."

Today wasn't like any
ordinary day. We were happy
not to travel the same
old way. We didn't know
those two women were
trying to get our
attention until we
turned our heads to the left.
Looking at them took our breath.
Their pretty Brown eyes, hypnotize.
their Peanut Butter skin, supreme
and energize, our stomachs
felt butterflies as their smiles
lifted us like the sunrise.
Their rides splendid. All
entertained our senses with
pleasure, so intended. They
are stunners! Just to think we
almost missed the opportunity to
get their numbers.

Sexy Swirls

We pulled over
to exchange contacts.
My friend and
and I were aroused by
their display of curves,
definitely adoring. We
weren't aware they
shook our hands, spoke
softly and said, "Call us
in the morning." We stood
there thinking we're out of
our lane our blush feelings cannot
be explained. We were strangers
like the night still we wanted
to kiss them convincingly at
first sight, and so we nodded our heads
in agreement excited with achievement.
We returned to our vehicles and thought
this is unbelievable. What is so weird about today,
about us feeling this way, we never thought we would
date Black girls until we met those beautiful Sexy Swirls.

Close Ties

"A good heart leads with its deeds. A good mind leads with its morality. A good spirit leads with its instinct. A good person leads with all to share their love."

As two walk with love
in harmony on a path that
measures forever,
the fate of life
brings them closer
to their endeavors.
The glare in their
eyes become the
sparkle of their hearts
the light in their hearts
knew not when love first start.

Easy laughter fills the corner or their minds as
love covers them through tough times. They ride
out the pathways to unveil what is true love's
glow in its
overflow.
The time
has come
for them
to unify
a symbol
of two as
one love
formalize
Close Ties.

Betrayal

> "What's interesting about broken trust is that you never detect when a person first betray you in their mind, but you will eventually see their behavior."

What we see and what we perceive in things and people are representations of our associations, interactions, and involvement with them. At the very basic of who we are, we are selective in behaviors and attitudes to communicate shared knowledge, information, and experiences.

As we learn to understand our actions, responses, and actualizations, it should not be to control others, but rather to empower and enrich lives through mature and nurturing relationships. Engagement in positive relationships can be meaningful, peaceful, beautiful, powerful, joyful, resourceful, and respectful.

Contrarily, relationships are not always what they seem. We can encounter people who foster a sense of psychological uneasiness, disturbance in behavior, or lack the capacity to channel negative emotions that are tied to the relentless facade of manipulation, selfishness, and self-defeating thoughts. People projecting poor psychological, behavioral, and emotional discomfort onto others should not be accepted but it's often tolerated.

We must be aware of what we project onto others and what others project onto us. The intensity of betrayal can be devastating and hurtful. Betrayal in any relationship is life's truth. Betrayal is like a compass for war on relationships. Its roots are usually associated with disconnection, deception, and relational violations. As life presents us with endless experiences, the reality is that we will always experience betrayal.

Poem Titles Narrative

When you are betrayed by those closest to you, you might say something like, *"Thought we were best friends, but little did I know....!"* From that point on you know nothing is going to be the same. You may feel hurt that the relationship ended but it's difficult to stay with someone who gives way to thinking like **I THOUGHT**. You may have been annoyed with someone who was a **COWARD ! Short on Fuel**, or had a **Limited Capacity** that lessens the chance for real connection and respect. In experiencing the manipulation of **Betrayal Blood** and **A Liar**, you know there will be **Fair Game!** You say to that person, *"You're Not Welcome Anymore*, it's a **Closed Chapter.**" That person writes a *"Letter to you: I'm Afraid."* Your response, *"A Year and A Day* is more than enough of your charade." You may have learned about **A Secret** and you're above dealing with **Many Wrongs**. At the end of the day, **Colors of Betrayal** will fall and not belong.

Thought we were best friends, but little did I know...!

"When you are unaware of betrayal, you'll contract yourself
out to a relationship of never knowing who and what you're getting."

She believed they
were closer than most.
She had her friend and her
husband. They always believed
in looking after each other sticking together
supporting each other. They experienced some ups
and downs for many rounds, but they always tried to reach new grounds.
She remembered the day when her friend looked in her eyes and told her she
was pregnant by some guy, a one night stand. It later turned out that guy was
an alibi for Ben. Yes, her husband then. Her memories counted the joyful times
she has been by her friend's side. While she demonstrated being a happy wife,
she helped her friend make plans to celebrate a new life. She invited her friend
into her home not knowing her friend and her husband were freaking on
her throne. Sometimes she fed her friend, even clothed her. She had sleepless
nights of shared secrets and listened to her friend's cries after. To her surprise,
her friend and her husband crept around with lies and laughter. When she found
out the child was her husband, her heart sunk, her thoughts were in a funk, she
had no spunk. She thought about getting drunk. Some said to forgive, others
said forgive not, revenge deserved a shot. She can't say she didn't give revenge
a thought. She was angry and distraught but it was nothing compared to the
abyss her friend and her husband fell into after the caught. She looked them
straight into their eyes, flaming with fire and said, "Thought we were best
friends, but little did I know...! you would fail me as a husband and you
would fail me as a friend. Both of you were truly my enemy in the end.
May God forgive you because it's not what I intend to do."

I THOUGHT

*"Emotional decisions can encourage an insensitive end.
Think to benefit more than yourself."*

I didn't want to hurt you. I know I

Took away what we needed the most and that was

Hope. I was drowning and I wanted a way

Out. I only cared about myself never anyone else. Not even our

Unity. I realized I was wrong. I suffered the consequences.

God told me, "He

Hates when I act like

That because he didn't raise me to be a brat but to obey." Now, I'm sorry I strayed.

COWARD!

"Getting involve with someone or something
when you're not ready can induce suffering."

People may choose someone unlike themselves. Their young minds force a
Collapse

they try to hide their incompetence, an inception Of

their intimidation, a product of pessimism, no Wisdom

they are frauds of many visions, backstabbers, and bleakness the same
Abandon

their blind strategies lack understanding of planning and no Real

sense of identity causing crash landings that make them neglect to honor
Devotion

The reason for this is they live life broken like a COWARD! in forward motion.

Short on Fuel

"Seek out relationships without letting yourself settle for less."

He reneged on sworn
oath to be the head. Instead,
he led as a proven leader of the dead.
He disappeared and sold his soul for underground
rewards to fulfill life with dishonest swords. He invested in
discord that nurtured destruction and carved no production.
His words traced from poison lips like no victory truth of an
enemy's ship that made history by cover ups and inflicted
torment intent. His iniquity bold as it robbed layers of
innocent arms recruited from
his selfish harms.

She had
enough of his interrupts.
He mentally exhausted her
like an angry
detainee but she
had to admit it
felt good to
be free like a
happy divorcee.
She knows when
he learns the golden rule
and stop being Short On Fuel
only then he can genuinely rule.

Limited Capacity

"Diligence can surpass issues that are brought forth by limitations."

They are annoyed
and trapped. They
both don't give a
crap. He does not
know what to do.
She cannot wait to
surrender to the truth.
Like a severe winter
storm hindering and
pushing in opposite
directions they can't
get along. His back is
against the wall. She is
tired of it all. Her regrets
her resentments are in the air.
She's feeling no care. He's angry he
can't meet her needs. He lied about doing
great deeds. He distanced himself from growth and
avoided what he can't be. They are tangled in thought
and let things fall where it's less fought. She no longer wanted
his touch because the lies grew too much, it was agony, apathy,
and he had the audacity to blame her for his Limited Capacity.

Betrayal Blood

"Betrayal has many faces. It does not have to be yours."

I didn't see it
coming. Misguided
emotions turned you
backwards. You played
out Judas. You lied, kissed
in distasted, vacated your post.
What a disgrace! Shame closed
your heart making matters worse from the start.
Constant blame turned to lies making matters worse in others' eyes.
Misery weighed heavily making matters worse steadily. Excuses were
useless making matters worse became a nuisance.
Disappointed in your tradeoff, too many
times with the same faceoff.
Now suffer your fate.
Your plunge awaits. I
live no more in the
darkness of your
outpours flowing
from the flood
of your
Betrayal
Blood.

A Liar!

*"A tongue that constantly lies respects no one.
It hates truth but honors deceit."*

Why do you lie so

making promises you can't

keep. How can you sleep? Telling women

it's you and them against the world (so cliché)

just to get their pearls. Do you expect them to believe

you when your actions lack conscious retrieval?
Why do you lie so
to come across as a
hero for others to
stroke your ego.
Do you expect
people to believe
you when your
actions are evil?
Why do you lie so
to impress others with
your grandiose. I guess
that's part of your diagnose.
Do you expect people to believe
you when your psyche is upheaval? Why do
you lie so about your status when evidence is debunked.
It's so unbecoming especially when you lack stability and long
funding. Do you expect people to believe you when your shifty ways
are illegal? Why do you lie so and tell others they can count on you
when you use every chance to show negative feedback as true.
Do you expect people to believe you? As A Liar!
your tongue is never peaceful, it's lethal.

Fair Game!

"What you give is what you will eventually receive."

Your dreams
came true to see
her face again.
Hold her
close again.
Love her to
the end. Still
you betrayed
her claiming it's not
intended but funny you often
offended. Your late nights
early mornings
travels to her side
thinking of all the
broken promises
breach trust and
commitment lies.

It made no sense
not to pull through. You 're frustrated
because you thought she invited someone else's shoes.
She gave her warning now she's gone she refused to take
it anymore. Look how you weep. You can't accept. You want
to reject images of her interlocked with another like bandages
healing wounds. Though she's not, she's just annoyed with your blind
spot. You should have stood your ground like a soldier. Instead, you had
no backbone and no composure. You reminisced about her smell, her eyes,
her presence, you hate to think someone else might be giving her lessons.
Your tears flowed like a river, you couldn't understand the pain it delivered.
Your ego's a mess. You know no rest, no peace. You're emotionally charged,
episodes discharged. You failed to regain her heart, it's such pain, but you
get no rewards for playing victim of a split brain. You should have
maintained to obtain her worth. Pain taught you next time
embrace the love you claim that's Fair Game!

You're Not Welcome Anymore

"Walking into someone's life with dishonest intent falsifies the relationship."

You trusted,
opened your
door to someone
you never thought to
almost destroy it all.
That someone
persuaded visions
of standing tall.
Advertisements claimed
delivery of
great installs.
Curtains went
up the show
started with an
electrifying applause.
Midway performance
curtains went down. You
were appalled by the fall.
Any good intentions
had no integrity
just withdraws.
You trusted,
opened your
door to someone
you never thought
to almost destroy
it all now you shut your
door to say to that someone
You're Not Welcome Anymore.

Closed Chapter

"The belief to trust a person is in the instinct of anticipated reciprocity but freeing yourself from that person is in the instinct of saving yourself."

Years have come and
gone leaving seasons warm
cold and storms. Feeling free
and strong, thoughts filled with
hopes, dreams, accomplishments so calm.

You think, "Why did I return to a path of unjustifiable harm?"

It's crazy to think there was
a chance to right the wrongs.
Clearly the writings were on the
walls, red flags and all. How could it be, thought
maybe this time there'll be no betrayal. No deceit.

You think, "Why did I return to a path of questionable heartbeat?"

But emptiness manifested
vulnerabilities to unwise senses, you should
have heeded memories of unhappy with playbook defenses.

You think, "Why did I return to a path of visible pretenses?"

You just had to walk through that door.
It made you wake up, picked your face up off
the floor. Though you learned no more! no more!

You think, "Why did I return to a path of infeasible restores?"

What matters now is that your eyes open wide.
Your heart played rewind. Your mind replayed in time.
God knows you didn't need snake eyes by your side to misalign.

You think, "Finally, I dismissed my downgrade as a
Closed Chapter bottom line!"

Letter to you: I'm Afraid

"Think before you do something that changes your position."

I never
wanted you to go.
I can't let no one
know you walked out
without reading my note.
I'm sorry I put my hands
around your throat.
I put on faces,
faked it. I convinced others we
made it. I never wanted you to go.
I can't let no one know you walked
out without saying goodbye. I know
I made mistakes but you too. I'm sorry
you caught me in lies. I put on faces,
faked it. I convinced others we saved
it. I never wanted you to
go. I can't let no one
know you walked out
without giving me
another chance. I know
I made mistakes
but you too. I'm sorry
I didn't apply. I ruined it all with
my masquerade. I should have prayed.
Now, I sit alone. I write a Letter to you:
I'm Afraid. I'm hesitant to tell others I
lost you. Where do I go? I really don't
want to hear them say, I told you so.

A Year and A Day

"For some, forgiveness is a choice.
For others, forgiveness is a requirement."

You pleaded
your need received
my deed and heed not
what we agreed. You
tried to lead me astray.
Took me for granted
every day. You
let matters give
way to unnecessary drama.
Rollercoaster emotions made it
difficult to stay and you felt that karma.
I was drained to understand your
display of plans.
Your low level
thinking crashed
at every chance.

A departure was
due clearly you weren't
full proof. I gave you many outs, still, you kept damaging the truth.
Too many mistakes and excuses are nothing but abuse. Your misleading
views are no longer a mystery. Guess What? Now, I can document that in
your case history. No qualms about you being a moron. It was best to
move on. My door is open for blessings, so long. A Year and A Day
no longer prolonged. I ended regrets of your yesterdays sad
songs. Though I learned to give, you learned to relive.
It's over now, be thankful I forgive.

A Secret

"Some things can only be concealed for a short time."

Heard
he's been
undercover. I
can't believe he's been in
denial all those years with
signs and messages shouting
out loud and clear. Heard he had
a Freudian slip or maybe it was simply
a conscious hint. How shameless to think
it's sexy to whisper in her ear a word Whites
should not share because Blacks wait to sue calling
it a racist cheer.
She called him out on what she heard, then he tried to
retract it by saying, "I didn't mean it like that, That's absurd!"
She knew what she heard that degrading word inappropriate at
the moment of her inviting him into her bed. What a blow to the head.
She might have forgiven him though if he would have told her he's tired of
living on the down low. He needs to stop being incognito. He needs to let her
know he's been frequently seeking below. She wondered about his onset
and he regretted living with A Secret.

Many Wrongs

"Guard yourself against people with negative energy."

It was at different times
and places when you welcomed others
into your space. There were no judgments of
their past but soon you saw they didn't belong
or had any appreciation for genuineness that could last.
They weren't forthright still you gave them the benefit of
the doubt without a fight. It might have been some time since
you opened the door to casual talk that offered commitment forever
more. Though, you should have ignored because later there was war
when you challenged their investment, but they couldn't handle that
assessment. Still, you gave acceptance to shared moments that
appeared truthful until developing factors were evident of
questionable behaviors as unusual. The experience became
an odyssey with too much dishonesty, perhaps they had
a positive toxicology.

Lies and darkness covered
the scene day and night you wanted
to scream. Their unresolved issues had you
given regular sessions once or twice, sometimes all week
advice, counseling their lost souls 'til twilight. It was official. They
despised you and emerged as artificial. They were delusional, their
brain lobes overload. They turned on you cold, started to probe, spread
gossip about you around the globe. They were saturated with self-doubt, they
denied that you honestly tried to help them with a way out. It was their darkness of unstable faith. Thankfully, you didn't make any of them your roommates. They flipped the switch with disgraceful utterance, a reveal of their sufferance. In the end, you refused to dumb down to their theatrics meltdowns. You walked away in your truth without bitterness but with indifference to the
Many Wrongs of ignorance.

Colors of Betrayal

"People who betray you are everywhere. You'll never know when they'll strike you, but they will fall."

You never treated them unkindly.
They didn't care that you portrayed gracefully,
peacefully, genuinely, professionally with a strong identity.
Their lack of integrity, expressions of bias and deceptive thoughts
and behaviors led a path throughout the years, throughout the months
as they plotted and schemed to dethrone. The evidence revealed itself
via phone, a day you never should have known. The darkness of envy,
jealousy, and insecurity are the fruits of their inferiority. Your presence
infuriated their spirits, so they advocated malicious intent as they waited
to make you feel devastated by the event. Your enemies formed an
allegiance, they smiled, thanked you, and pretended to support you
even though they hated you. What they secretly planned at your
expense never gave you a chance for true defense. They thought
less of you as they hoped to celebrate your fall through. Their
vicious ways removed you from the small town, but they can
never take away your crown. Here comes the countdown,
the universe turned things around. One by one, low
and high, they began to face the showdown. It was
vengeance above that shook the ground making
them pay for the intended harm around and
around. Sometimes discovering the
Colors of Betrayal lets you know
who's unstable, who sits at
your table, who you need
to label, more importantly
who you need to disable.

An Invested You

"The wills of our deeds impact aspects of our lives.
What's in our hearts and spirits will determine the returns in our lives."

Our environments can influence how we think and feel, what we value and believe, and what can peak our interests, connectedness, and wholeness to be as good as the desire perceived. If we continuously engage in anything that controls our thinking, then our behavior will shadow it. If we are not invested in our growth, living can become a dangling residue of hope or temporary upgrades that often fade out to small imaginations and superficial deeds.

In our self-investment, we can stretch our thinking to evaluate opportunities for strategic change. This change can come from knowledge and information that come from wisdom and imagination that come from learning experiences of making mistakes. Having Knowledge, Information, Wisdom, and Imagination, what I call "KIWI" ingredients, are specks of growth that widen our significance.

Over time, self-investment should be a safety net for being true to who we are without someone else defining our skin, our culture, and our images. When we learn to break the psychological, emotional, and spiritual chains from what I call the "SYSTEM," Selling Your Soul To Enemy's Manipulation, then it's possible to reach new heights of vibrant living for building healthy minds, environments, and relationships.

Poem Titles Narrative

When you Find Yourself to discover *The Butterfly Within* and move *Like Eagle Wings*, you are *Living to Know You* are not *Alone in a crowd*. Your **Invisible Ropes** are in your *Alphabet Soul: A confirmation seal* that lets you know that *God Got Your Back!* because you are made a *Lovely You*. The *Black Man* stands with purpose to embrace *Shades of Beautiful,* an inclusion of *CIA Beauty*. The many things that impact you and others like you because of the symptoms of the environment make you think, *I Walk a Path* to understand *One and Many*. To my God, *I Salute You!* in *Music and Me* because *God Only Knows, Where My Footsteps Lead* through *Doorways: A chosen way*. In continuous thought you think others don't know what it's like to *Walk In My Shoes* for *A New Start* and to rethink about *The Greatest Gift Used To Control*. You have to take steps to *Unplug the Program* and *Never Stay A Victim*. You think over and over, *Still They Know* that *LIFE* means everything to be *Black Again* regardless of the hate and ignorance against my skin. And so, in the beginning, God and Goddess said let there be *AFRICA* and *That's My Word*!

Find Yourself

*"Only you can live your purpose.
Don't let someone else make you their puppet."*

You search for clarity of who you need to be as a future achiever. You say to yourself, "I need to become a wise leader." But you let doubt and meager grab your ears as a booster to fear what you cannot vision on destiny meter. Stand firm. Shut down that demon speaker trying to steal your demeanor. Keep your voice as your teacher reminding you to take on your future with meaning wisdom, patience, and knowledge but the ultimate is as a believer. Back on track you humor the foundation of your mission saying, "As a contender, sooner than tomorrow my destiny is no longer a rumor but as a ruler knowing purpose cannot rise without passion adventures." This makes you welcome the pressures that measure to Find Yourself is to rediscover you are indeed a treasure.

The Butterfly Within

"Life pushes out the old to become a new birth."

I live on ground. I want to move up
and around to find a place unknown to
my current position, one of a new mission
through brilliant transition. I live on ground.
I need to get out of my cocoon to become
a different me under the high moon.
Tell me what else is there to
learn when steady flow is
engage in its plateau?
Perhaps, the time
comes for an
outgrowth
breaking
status quo.
I live on ground.
I'm feeling indecisive.
Some say it's a midlife crisis
or going through changes. That's a possibility
playing out in stages making things rearranged. I live on ground.
I have an urge exploding inside. Nature enforced its time. The clock
chimed. I can't help but take to the wind and fly like The Butterfly Within.

Like Eagle Wings

"Your existence will not fade when you exit on ground
that's when you surge towards survival."

Be
beautiful
wings like an
eagle's spread
gliding blue skies
climbing white clouds
high. Be beautiful wings
like an eagle's swooping dive eagle eyeing its target scooping the opportunity
alive. Be beautiful wings like an eagle's independence, concentration, and
abundance survive. Be beautiful wings like an eagle's open wide
living, soaring to its fullest thrive. Be beautiful wings
like an eagle's
fearlessness
and tenacity
with masterful
drive. Be beautiful
wings Like Eagle Wings
flying with purpose and
freedom through its eyes.

Living to Know You

"Know yourself. Love yourself."

Living is
learning your true history.
Living is
learning what is true liberty.
Living is
understanding your burdens.
Living is
understanding that nothing is
for certain.
Living is
fulfilling your milestones as your own.
Living is
fulfilling your worth without postpone.
Living is
looking at what consumes you.
Living is
looking at what improves you.
Living is
being aware when to change course.
Living is
being aware of the Trojan Horse.
Living is
knowing your identity.
Living is
knowing at the end of the day you are
Living To Know You
through serenity.

Alone in a crowd

"To feel alone is not being lonely. It is being an individual."

I'm in a crowd

loud with laughter

waves of energy sought after

still I feel empty still I feel alone.

I'm in a crowd with significant

minds serving its kind still

I feel empty still I feel alone.

I'm in a crowd

celebrated by versatile fans admiring my

signature brand still I feel empty still I feel alone.

I'm in a crowd joined in hands with shouters

and praise dancers still I feel empty still I feel alone.

I'm in a crowd with closed eyes and meditated minds

unconfined. I'm no longer empty. I'm no longer

Alone in a crowd. I am an individual
who is connected to the universe
energy endow.

Invisible Ropes

"Feed your spirit the ingredients it needs to make yourself whole."

The
capacity
of your
motivation is
to focus your
vision on things
that support
you and on

people who

support your truth...

Your truth must align with

new thinking that transforms your spirit...

Your spirit is in your worth to give and receive possibilities...

Your possibilities are the way to bring forth insights in your fight...

Your fight is in your acknowledgement of failures but honor rewards...

Your rewards are to share knowledge and not waste time to be made whole...

Your whole is in the qualities that shaped your hopes connected to your

Invisible Ropes.

Alphabet Soul: A confirmation seal

"Count on your higher spirit to see you through.
Count on yourself to carry you through."

The Alphabet
of your soul delivers you
from shadows below. The Alphabet
of your soul delivers you successful outflows.
The Alphabet of your soul delivers morals as you
grow. The Alphabet of your soul delivers what you sow.
The Alphabet of your soul delivers you as your commando.

(A) Anyone who
   (B) Believes in the
      (C) Creator to be
         (D) Divine will
            (E) Embrace
(F) Freedom   (G) Greatness
   (H) Healing
      (I) Integrity
         (J) Justice

   (K) Kindness
      (M) Meaning
         (N) Nurturing
            (O) Opportunity
(P) Peace
  (Q) Quality
     (R) Righteousness
        (S) Spirituality
          (T) Truth
             (U) Unity
               (V) Victory and
                  (W) Wisdom
                     as these are
                       (X) X-Rays in
                        (Y) Your
                          (Z) Zeal

It's your Alphabet Soul: A confirmation seal.

God Got Your Back!

"When chaos finds its way in you,
seek help to remove it."

Stop standing
in the middle of the
road looking crazy. How
did you get here? I hear
your Heart racing. Look up!
God will act.

Stop standing in
the middle of the road looking
crazy. How did you let someone
take you there? Don't continue to
lose your way. Look Up!
God will contact.

Stop standing in
the middle of the
road looking crazy.
What have you
done to your self-care?
You have to get out
of this mess. Look up!
God will impact.

Stop standing in the middle of the
road looking crazy. And so, you ask,
"Where do I go in despair?" You find prayer.
Move. Breathe. Push back. Look up!
God Got Your Back!

Lovely You

"You have beauty that speaks for itself."

Looking at the sky, it's beautifully blue

        Heavenly God blessed it true.

Looking at you, engage in your smile

        Heavenly Goddess blessed you as you grew.

Looking into your eyes, so hypnotized

        Heavenly God blessed your view.

Looking into your spirit, a greatness through

        Heavenly Goddess blessed you as she knew.

Looking at the glow and the power of your skin, nothing protects it more like the melanin within and no copy can undo what the

        Heavenly God and Goddess blessed as a Lovely you.

Black Man

"Who you are and what you give becomes your legacy."

Black Man
like Imhotep you walk
with peace though you pose a
threat to those who know your
height of mind is like a mass
production that leaves
others behind.
Black Man
like Imhotep you stand like the
Pyramids in Kemet beyond what others can
fathom or imagine. Black Man like Imhotep
you build your home with depth like
the King you are who
steps first with the
left showing you
are a warrior who
protects his Queen
with prep. Black Man
like Imhotep when you feel
you have to protest a worthy cause
know that you are of the finest creation
that represented like Imhotep, a man of skills and
brilliance who led life   with will and resilience.

Shades of Beautiful

"The beautiful, the bold, and
the brilliant start with the Black."

Women,
Shades of Beautiful
Don't dispute. Know who you are.
You come too far. Achievable, Spiritual, Intellectual.
Your features and physique strong others mimicking to belong.

Women,
Shades of Beautiful
Don't dispute. Know who you are.
You come too far. Respect yourselves. No need to
compromise your position. You are already above the competition.
Your features and physique strong others mimicking to belong.

Women,
Shades of Beautiful
Don't dispute. Know who you are.
You come too far. Hold your heads up high but
not in arrogance. You are Incredible, Irresistible, Influential.
Your features and physique strong others mimicking to belong.

Women,
Shades of Beautiful
Don't dispute. Know who you are.
You come too far. You are unforgettable. Never
think you're invisible. You are contemporary, memorable.
Your features and physique strong others mimicking to belong.

Women,
Shades of Beautiful
Don't dispute. Know who you are.
You come too far. Don't uplift yourselves by the
enemies' agenda. Love yourselves in your image not
in copies or pretenders. You are Original. Historical.
Biblical. That means you are Beautiful Black African Queens.
Your features and physique strong others mimicking to belong.

CIA Beauty

"The marvel of you give energy to others."

There

you

are,

covering the

world as you stretch

the imagination delicately yet strongly

holding many eyes with your colorful sophistication talents

and gifts making many wish and persist to make your guess list.

There you are, your radiant warmth shining like a sizable diamond that

make others welcome you because you are absolutely and truly known as

Caribbean

Indian

African

Beauty.

I Walk a Path

"The guidance of your path can lead to
many decisions to know yourself."

I walk a path
where I stop
to look back only to
stare in a mirror of
images changed and
no one knows the

many faces that came. I

walk a path where I stop

to look back only to walk

forward to know one and the

same. I walk a path where I stop

to look back only to fall victim to life's

lessons without knowingly gains. I walk

a path where I stop to look back

only to accept the truth of living forward

with no more shame. I Walk a Path

where I can be complete in my name.

One and Many

"All things in life are not meant to strengthen you.
Some things are meant to breakdown your defensives.
It's up to you to build your strengths."

Who are you?
I am a member who don't
know what to do. Just don't know how to
navigate through the transition of experiences to be
true to you. Who are you? I am a role who don't know
what to do. Just don't know how to navigate through the
transition of experiences to be true to you. Who are you?
I am a man. I am a woman. I am a child who don't know
what to do. Just don't know how to navigate through
the transition of experiences to be true to you.

Who are you? I am you who don't know what
to do. Just don't know how to navigate through
the transition of experiences to be true to you.
Who are you? I am enslaved mentalities
behaviors, emotions, and spirits that don't
know what to do. Just don't know how
to navigate through the transition of
experiences to be true to you.

Who are you?
I am One and Many
who are diverse and internally
struggles. Just don't know what to do.
Just don't know how to navigate through the
transition of experiences to be true to you, except
through my own image to be true to you and me.

I Salute You!

"We are given different gifts to help others upgrade their lives and our own."

Oh, God! Goddess!

I sometimes get worrisome.
I sometimes want to run.
I sometimes am confused.
I sometimes feel used.

I sometimes think things are funny.
I sometimes think people are really dummies.
I sometimes think I need to make a change.
I sometimes feel that things are prearranged.
I sometimes feel life is difficult, theoretical.
I sometimes feel my life needs a miracle.

Oh, God! Goddess!

On another note,
I feed the hungry. I shelter the homeless.
I help an average man. I help survivors of abused hands.
I donate time to charity. I donate time to families.
I visit the old. I visit the young.
I visit prisoners who were and are drug strung.
I serve others comfortably. I serve the environment humbly.

Oh, God! Goddess!

On another note,
I continue to pray. Thank you for showing me the way.
Being human is not easy on any day. Without your grace, life is impossible to help others, correct my mistakes, and see things through so I Salute you!

Music and Me

"The spirit dances to the rhythm of the feet and deepens the mind of the soul."

Synergy of
music and me
undeniably agree.
Feel the beat kinetic whine.
Synergy of music and me
a dancing spree. Feel the beat energetic
incline. Synergy of music and me like a family
tree. Feel the beat through its bloodline.
Synergy of music and me wide
like the sea. Feel the beat
magnetic combine.
Synergy of music
and me full
of glee.
Feel the
beat
poetic
minds.
Synergy of
music and me
completely free.
Feel the beat aesthetic align.
Synergy of music and me appease thee.
Feel the beat in its spine. Synergy of Music and Me
never miss a beat because it's God and Goddess' design.

God Only Knows

"What we want to know is not always what we
can or might be willing to comprehend."

Astonish by
white clouds glow as
it embellish my heart
smooth and comfortable
in my spiritual start. I must cherish
its development, its freedom of thoughts,
its energy of life flowing purposeful as
it's changeable in flight day and night.

I want to
know what lies
under/above
white clouds glow
but God Only Knows
a moment in time taken,
escaping my mind beyond
limitless space, division of lines
design. I want to know what lies
under/above white clouds glow
but God Only Knows visions
sufficiently bestow from
substance of nature,
a profound element
pulling-pushing
direction possibly
end as a favor.

I want to know what lies
under/above white clouds glow but
God Only Knows the whispers echo in the
distance as our elevation and resilience are
courage instruments position for a mission.
I want to know what lies under/above white
clouds glow but God Only Knows.

Where My Footsteps Lead

"Sometimes uncertainty happens until steps of
self-maintenance are outlined for productive solutions."

Shadows

of my footsteps

move while my mind is

restless in place trying to escape

the images and feelings I must replace.

My footsteps move forward and backward in a race, but
it really does not matter that I cannot change the way they
have known its haste. It's too late to erase the errors of
their mistakes. I must contemplate the chase.
I cannot doubt its place to recognize
what they have traced.

What it all means is that

I must understand Where My Footsteps

Lead, sometimes near or far, is the fate of its pace.

I must keep thinking, keep moving, keep challenging

the challenge even when I fall short of balance.

Doorways: A chosen way

"What is asked in your spirit with sincerity can open doors."

I walk through
the doorways
to search for the unknown.
I walk through the doorways
of desires condone.
I walk through the doorways
to see who cares.
I walk through the doorways
of vivid nightmares.
I walk through the doorways
of multiple dreams.
I walk through the doorways
of mirrors placed
before me.
I walk through
the doorways
of hidden secrets.
I walk through the doorways of
weaknesses and incompleteness.
I walk through the doorways to confront my meaning.
I walk through the doorways to seek us and Black Jesus.
I walk through the Doorways: A chosen way
to be deepened in my spiritual Eden.

Walk In My Shoes

"The judgment from others is common.
Don't concern yourself with hypocrites."

You don't know me　　　but you judge me.
I walk a thousand miles a day
that's just in my head.
I walk a thousand
miles a day
beating my-
self up
feeling
scared.

You don't know me　　　but you judge me.
I walk a thousand miles a day
for something special
instead. I walk a
thousand miles a
day watching
people being
mislead.

You don't know me　　　but you judge me.
I walk a thousand miles a day
for a breakthrough. I
walk a thousand
miles a day
not to be
subdue.

You don't know me　　　but still you judge me.
You don't know what it's
like to Walk
In My Shoes
just to stay
ahead of all
that accuse.

A New Start

"To prosper is to make change through
planning and action not just talk."

I beat the night.
Sunrises in my face bright.
My eyes dry. Need healing apply.
I move my feet. Want no more bad energy repeats.
I hurt no more. Time to explore a world better than before.
I got rid of strife. Have to enjoy life. My higher spirit, I'm coming for
A New Start, a renew heart. Help me to stay true. I trust in you.

On my knees thanking you
even overseas. My
hands raise
giving you
spiritual
praise.
Dip me
in water.

I am your daughter.
I am your son. I know your truth is
above man-made. I pray only to you not
the one that's falsely portrayed. Lead the
way. I am yours to command every day.

The Greatest Gift Used To Control

"A people who are stripped of their origin must learn again who they are through their spirit, ancestors, and self-knowledge."

There was a
time when the soil
beneath our feet made us
grow with nutrients from the sunbeam
feeding our dark skin that many wanted
and still do as they also deny that our bloodstream runs through.
We had fun with our kind. We built cultural signs and a way of life.

We created guidelines. We developed strong minds, bodies, and spirituality through pineal gland vitality, the universe stars and astronomy, and Gods and Goddesses economy. We were feeling free not knowing any harm of any degree until one day there was a split in the family's personality tree. Visitors came and presented a gift with deceitful intervene as most welcomed and believed, some were inattentive and failed to receive.

They gave us their bible that made us not
see, made us bleed, made us more in need. We
can't recognize our own we are confused. They
gave us their bible and many got caught in the
noose and they didn't want us to reproduce.

They made us fall. They made us broken. They gave us
their bible to convince us we'll be closer and better than
before as long as we live up to a new name that they brought forth.
As a people, we are spiritual. We gave them back their bible we want the
original, the biblical without fictional. They gave us their bible for us to use
against ourselves, no longer knowing thyself. They took our survival and hunt
us like prey with The Greatest Gift Used To Control us and many obey.

Unplug the Program

"You are only as elevated as the company you keep
and the information and images you receive."

Why accept
superficial change it's nothing more than backward
thinking, an induced mind sinking. Can't you hear the bells ringing.
Don't you see the conditioning through symbols for you to salivate at
what they want you to resemble. Stop committing suicide by psychological
death denying your mental strengths, support, and self-worth because
of self-hate living up to the expectations of the oppressors' design bait.
Stop committing suicide by physical death denying your nose, lips, hips,
hairstyles stiff, and whitening and lightening to fit in because of
self-hate living up to the expectations of the oppressors' design bait.
Can't you hear the bells ringing. Don't you see the conditioning
through symbols for you to salivate at what they want
you to resemble. It's a trick. They're injecting
their lips and hips and burning
themselves to look like
our hieroglyphs.

Stop
committing suicide by
emotional and spiritual death denying
your balance, connectedness, and energy
because of self-hate living up to the expectations
of the oppressors' design bait. Stop committing suicide
by origin death denying your identity and powerfulness as
you harm, kill, degrade and enslave each other for practice be-
cause of self-hate living up to the expectations of the oppressors'
design bait. Can't you hear the bells ringing. Don't you see the
conditioning through symbols for you to salivate at what they want
you to resemble. Stop committing suicide by denying you are above.
Break the self-hate, deactivate the oppressors' designed brainwash bait.
If you keep loving your enemies' scams, you will never
Unplug The Program.

Never Stay A Victim

"Anyone who stays stuck to enslavement, stays a victim
to justifying their complacency and situation."

Why are

you still serving

like a slave? Don't

you remember how far

we've come, how

far we've run

to know our way.

They try to tell us we're
all the same. That can't be.
There is never equality in a
system that takes our freedom,
language, culture, and imagination
while they rob and rape our men, women,
and children believing we were worthless from
the beginning. We will never be equal when we are
a diverse people of goals, needs, education, destinations,
coping, revolutions, and sequels. We must love ourselves
and move away from control help, control isms, find wisdom.
Never Stay A Victim.

Still They Know

"Those who know they are not an equal people
will plot against those who threatens their survival."

They said we
had no name. They said we had no intelligent brain. They said
we had animal characteristics running wild but it's funny that
they were savages who craved and stole our styles. They said
we never navigated the seas. They said we never could
read. They said we never had goals but it's
funny that they craved and stole our
sophisticated scrolls. They said we
were slaves. They said we
were less than nothing
and slain millions
of us to the grave
and claimed the
rest needed to
be saved but it's
funny that they
craved, stole,
and raised our
spiritual praise.
They said we will forever
be chained. They said we will
forever know no escape. They said
we are a hated race but it's funny that
they still crave our origin they whitewashed
to recreate their own while secretly bowing down
to us because Still They Know we are their home.

LIFE

"Balance is what gives meaning to life."

Who I am of my own is
what I become because of the
ancestors who sat on the throne.
Although scattered to a foreign land
on borrowed time   how can I repay
the Creator who   breathed in my
kind before any other   human-kind, except
pay not as a fool   but in obedience
of my ways that   follow in the rules
over my heart   over my mind
over my eyes over my body over my soul.
Ancestors, the light of the Creator, you were the strength
of Kemet who overcame boundaries and limits. Though I live
in no perfect way still I live to practice the best during my days.
My footsteps strive
in our greatness
and of the spirit
to be uplifted
by our ethnicity
birth of notable
histories and
contemporary
memories which
push through to
my consciousness
my experiences my
culture my thinking
as I embrace it all for
my understanding that
Learning is for my focus.
Intimacy is for my balance.
Freedom is for my mentality.
Energy is for my spirituality and
LIFE from my kind gave to humanity.

Black Again

"Be proud to be an original. Be proud to be you."

If I am to be
born again in another life,
God, please make me as I am, Black.
As Black, my senses move toward the
horizon like the bright and beautiful
stars that pull me into the mouth
of the spirit. If I am to be born
again in another life, God, please
make me as I am, Black. As Black, I am inherit, I'm
looking through the black mirrors to see all who oppose
me yet adore me because I am free. Yes free that's why
they fight me so hard to take the lead and using my
stories as creed.
If I am to be born
again in another life,
God, please make me as
I am, Black. As Black, I am
whole like the seed of dark
matter that spreads as
wide hands that grasp
to mold thick layers
of the Black Land.
If I am to be born
again in another life,
God, please make me
as I am, Black. As Black,
I am of favor like the sun
adorn shining like royalty born.
If I am to be born again in another life,
God, please make me as I am, Black. As Black,
I am the sound of many horns that ripple through skies
like thunder roaring with strength, power, and wonder. If I am
to be born again in another life, God, please make me as I am, Black.
As Black, I am a lover of my skin color which is Godsend like that to ascend as
Black Again.

AFRICA

"AFRICA, the birthplace where the Creator made no mistakes to start the human race."

Absolute eminence.

First to give life, a true Genesis.

Rich in meaning, spirituality, and energy.

Intellectual minds offered Ma'at laws for living in synergy.

Civilization beyond others, well educated, liberated, and illustrated in

Advance creativities that were and still admired. AFRICA, the start of life where others hate to authenticate, but they stolen and imitated many of Black Africans' concepts, stories, symbols of laws, Pyramids, Eye of Horus and RA, monuments, and temples as they also defaced Black Africans' initials. The greatness in AFRICA was too civil and that made them feel little.

That's My Word!

"From the energy above we were born to live in the light of love."

Look at them
They are immutable, wonderful,
spiritual, truthful, never expendable. They
will discover you. Adore you. Shine their
light on you. Put no one above you. How can they
let you go? They want to hold you so. All wrapped
up ready to show you their love. Don't depart when
they want you the most to fulfill your part. They
would never double cross you like the many
times you crossed them. They just want
you to build strong character
through their networks trying to
save you regrets.
They want to teach you reach you
not preach to you. They are not going to
plead with you just know when you leave them
you will feel fear as they announce your despair.
Dare them not to share that side of your healthcare.
You really don't want them to take it there. They are
brave always letting you know they are here to
stay. Thought you would want it that way.
If you take away their love today,
don't wait until tomorrow
to stray your space. About face
for they will seek another to be
true. They always do. Look at
them. They are sometimes
disputable by many who
are uncomfortable that
they made you, me, and
our ancestors so
affirmable, remarkable.
Maybe one day you might
believe that our Gods and
Goddesses are above all.
They created us from
love to be preferred
That's My Word!

ADDICTIONAL PERSONAL QUOTES

"Love and respect yourself. Get to know who you are. Grow to appreciate yourself and others."

"Validation should come from a special place within."

"Freedom of the mind is the commander and chief. If you fail to protect your mind, then you fail to protect everything else that follows."

"Change is to the mindset like Knowledge is to the strengthen mind like Self is to the known identity."

"We are all coded."
"Every hand does not have your best interest."
"What's in your mind and spirit will manifest. Don't let jealousy get the best of you."
"People eat what consumes them."
"Pleasures will cost you."
"As Pride, It's all about me."

"We all contribute to something, but it does not have to be negative. Break the hate."
"Sometimes life fight back."
"Thoughts and situations affect us differently. Help others to help themselves."
"Just when you think you have it under control, think again."

"What you give represents who you are."
"Grow beyond your circumference."
"The life of the mind can open wide with expressions of energy."

"Desires are personal."
"And so, it starts…"
"Sometimes nothing good follows sorry."
"When you are more than excuses, then it's possible to win."

"Find that safe place in your spirit."
"The range of our understanding is not beyond the Creator."
"Getting to know the Higher Spirit is not the problem. It's knowing that man's words are not trusting."
"An enslaved mind will never know it can be free."
"Come together to birth greatness."
"There is such joy when you know who you are."
"The truth always leaves its mark."

www.ingramcontent.com/pod-product-compliance
Lightning Source LLC
Chambersburg PA
CBHW051944160426
43198CB00013B/2292